Mommy's Reflections

ZUTON LUCERO-MILLS

Mommy's Reflections

Cover photo courtesy of the Denver Post.
Photographer Hyoung Chang.

ISBN-13: 978-0-9824255-6-5
ISBN-10: 0-9824255-6-2

I witnessed the miracle of life as I watched Zumante being born. I supported my sister as she moaned and screamed and cried and yelled and pushed and demanded the epidural that it was too late to give her. I saw that pain give way to pure joy and exhausted exhilaration as Zumante, Zuton's first child, was placed into her arms. She was in awe of him. From that moment on I watched Zuton indulge his desires, invest in his education and plan for his future.

We never imagined that less than ten years later, his life would tragically end. As parents we don't expect to outlive our children. We provide for them in our wills and life insurance policies, we relay to them our last wishes and instructions for our burials. We try to prepare them for our departure because surely, inevitably, they will know life without us. It is a reasonable expectation. It is the natural order of life. Whenever that does not happen, when there is a violation of the natural order and a child stops breathing, the pain is overwhelming.

I am certain that there is no greater tragedy, no more devastating loss than the death of a child. Particularly when that casualty is preventable, when the negligence or callousness of others results in the demise of our own children, the pain is especially intense. When Zumante passed I saw a light go out in my sister's eyes that to this day has never fully returned. She is forever changed by this loss, the horrific experience of losing her son. Nonetheless, when Zumante joined the Egun (ancestors), my sister continued to mother him. She created rituals to nurture his spirit. She told his story to laymen and lawmakers in the hope of encouraging health care reform so that no other mother would have to suffer the loss that she did. She sacrificed to ensure that Zumante did not die in vain.

Most parents would refer to the pain of losing a child as indescribable; a persistent and overwhelming feeling that is beyond words. In this book, Zuton has managed to articulate the unspeakable. She has taken the journal entries from the days, weeks and months following Zumante's transition and transformed them into an insightful piece of literature. She has shared her most painful, personal and complex thoughts. In writing this book, Zuton has attempted to hasten her own healing. Some people say that time heals all wounds. Others know that work heals wounds and that prayer and time facilitate that process. In writing this book, Zuton has done much of that healing work for herself. She has taken control of her own therapeutic process and shared it with the world in honor of her son.

If you have lost a child, this book will help you. If you want to support someone whose child has passed, this book will enlighten you. If you have experienced any other kind of hurt or loss this book will inspire you. No matter what your circumstance, this book will encourage you to face your challenges with courage, nurture your relationships with love and integrity and live your life to the fullest.

I share deeply in the loss of Zumante and I grieve for the part of my sister that left with him. Although I share in this loss, I am mindful of the fact that for his mother, the one who carried him in her womb for nine months, nursed him for twelve, and mothers him still that the pain is much deeper. I know that Zumante chose Zuton to be his mother. I am grateful for having benefited from that choice and I am honored to be his Titi. Even in spirit, Zumante is doing the revolutionary work of fighting injustice, hastening human rights and making the world a better place.

In any challenging situation, in the loss of Zumante, there are lessons to be learned. The lessons for me are profound. If my baby sister can bury her son, nurture his spirit, establish a foundation in his name, tend to his grave site, fight for health care reform in his honor, tend to the community garden in his memory, go to work, be supportive of her spouse, raise her surviving children, help them with their homework, ensure that they are all performing well above grade level, take them to dance class, attend their basketball games, drive them to Karate lessons, go to weekly therapy with them and write a book; then surely, I can get through the painful losses and stressors in my life. I don't know what the lessons in this book will be for you. I am certain that you will grow from reading it.

There is an African (Yoruba) proverb that states, "A kì í bẹ̀rù ikú bẹ̀rù àrùn ká ní kí ọmọ ó kú sinni. No one fears death or disease more than the loss of her child". In living through Zumante's passing, Zuton has courageously faced a parent's deepest fear. I honor her struggle, and I share her hope that no other mother has to endure what she has; what she does every day. I support her in every way that I can. It is my hope that you will support her by ensuring the basic human right to adequate health care, and by reading this book. Thank you in advance for doing both.

~Olisa Yaa Tolokun-Ajinaku, MS, LPC, CACP

Dear Reader,

At this time in my life, it is my personal belief that losing a child to death is the hardest thing in the world. I suppose that the possibility exists that there is, in fact, something more difficult. If that is the case, I sincerely hope to never encounter it. Each day for me is a Herculean task. Every day routines are not routine anymore. However, this book is important to me. It has truly been a labor of love. I expect that, sometimes, this may be a hard read, but it has been a hard write and a hard experience. If you are attempting to navigate the death of your own child; please know that in the darkest of moments, when you have never felt more alone, others have felt what you are feeling. And if you live on the other side—if you have no firsthand knowledge of such things—I hope that you are able to gain insight.

I am one mother. No two experiences can be exact duplicates. Therefore, this is my story from my perspective. It is just one Mommy's Reflections.

This is for you, Zumante.

In the beginning...

The moment that I found out that I was pregnant with my first child, I burst into tears. I had just withdrawn from college after two years, and I hadn't quite formulated my life's plan. I had thought I was ready to be a mother—had, in fact, wished for it fervently. Now that my wish was apparently being granted, I was in a panic. So, I cried. It was awhile before the idea of motherhood regained its appeal, but once it did, I was fairly giddy with joy.

On August 14, 1999, Zumante was born. I loved him, and nurtured him, and tried to cultivate his growth. He, in turn, loved me, and nurtured me, taught me and forced me to grow.

It seems to me that being a mother is the most amazing, terrifying, dizzying, exhilarating, challenging, wondrous thing on earth. I have felt both punished and privileged.

Zumante died on July 20, 2009. I am blessed to be his mother. These are some of my reflections.

There are no words that would be sufficient in expressing myself. It is with this knowledge that I make the attempt to do so anyway... for my son.

September 18, 2009

The day you were born was one of many different emotions for me. Most significant was after you were delivered and had been placed in my arms. I felt such an overwhelming love. I never knew it was possible to love that way. I immediately decided that I shouldn't have any more children because I felt that nothing could surpass my love for you, my firstborn. You simply amazed me. I took you home and watched you and never wanted you out of my sight. When you cried, I cried too. I never stopped.

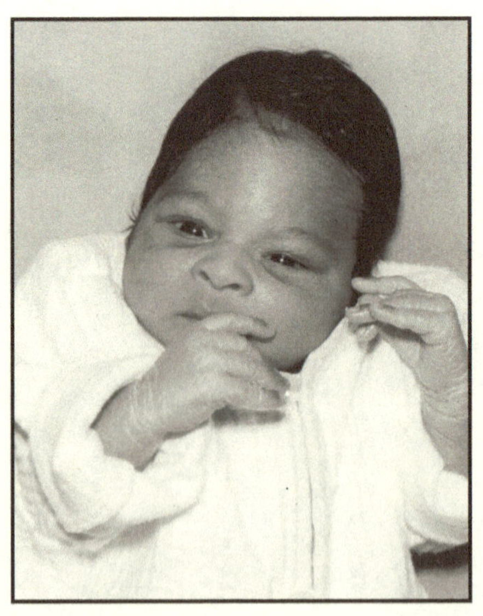

It is very nearly impossible to describe the emotions a woman experiences upon becoming a mother. It is an amazing thing. The love I had encountered prior to motherhood could not begin to compare with the new level of love I discovered when Zumante was born. I know of nothing that can rival a woman's love for her child.

September 18, 2009

The day you died, my soul was in torment. I had such a hard time bringing you into this world—I didn't think I could get you here. And I knew that I had to let you leave this world, and I didn't think I could do that either. It seemed like so many other times over your life, when I doubted my ability to do for you. Yet, I did my best. I still am.

Zumante had been in the hospital for several days. He was not getting better. I had been charged with the impossible task of deciding whether he should remain on the ventilator. I paced the hospital corridors, and cried, and prayed. I felt helpless and weak. But I somehow did what had to be done. When you are a mom, it comes with the territory.

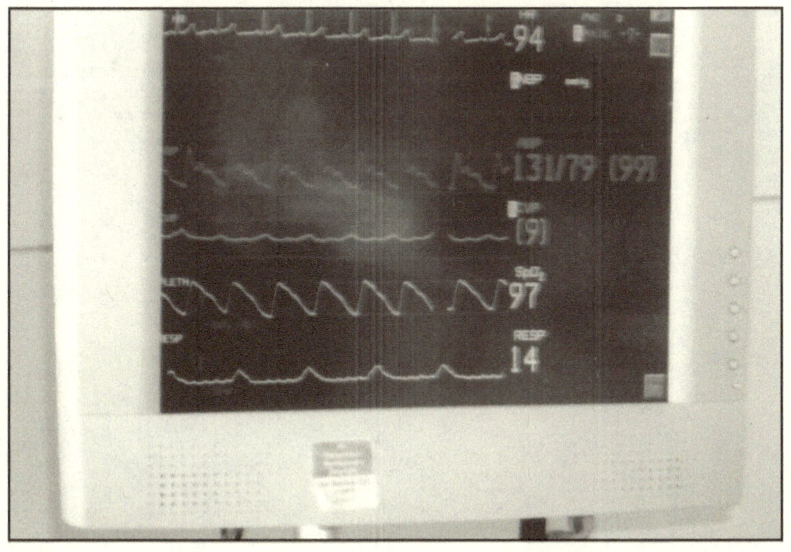

September 18, 2009

The other day, Dreamgirls was on TV. The other kids watched it, and I sat behind them and cried. After they went to bed, I remembered that your favorite song from the movie was Patience. I am trying to have it.

The Bible says that patience is a virtue. I have always been proud of my ability to be patient. But after Zumante died, it wasn't so easy. I had no patience with a world that would take a son from his mother…but Zumante had tried to be patient. I figured that if he could try, I certainly could.

September 18, 2009

Yesterday, I saw some of your artwork. It was titled "The Snake of Courage." I wondered. Did you know that I would need it?

Courage is a challenging thing to have. When your child dies, courage is something you need desperately. It intrigued me when I saw Zumante's art panel. I knew that he had struggled and labored to create it. I wondered if he had visions of what the future held. I suppose he must have battled against his own snake of courage. In the end, though, in his last moments of consciousness, I could tell he was afraid. I was too. Often, I still am. I try to think of courage as a snake—often lying in wait until it becomes necessary to rear its head—and then becoming a force to contend with. A snake. Power. Courage.

September 18, 2009

I sometimes think that you taught me so much more than I taught you. I'm still learning from you—even now.

When I became a mother, I looked forward to teaching my child a great many things. I suppose I succeeded in doing that. What I didn't anticipate was how much I would learn. I really did learn a great many things in kindergarten. The rest of what I needed to learn, I am learning from being a mommy. Children are not only our students, they are our teachers.

September 18, 2009

Your sister told me that she is mad that God took you away. I told her that I am too. One of my first thoughts was "What God in his right mind would think that anyone can bear this?" But then I remember that for almost two months now, you haven't itched. You haven't had to look out for peanut butter. You haven't had to stop playing before you were ready. You haven't had to take a breathing treatment. And I am grateful.

Anger is a part of grief. Sometimes, it is one of the more bearable parts. It lends itself nicely to quiet fuming and screams of indignation. It feels more useful than sadness even if it really isn't.

Reflection is another part of grief. When Zumante died, I pondered the things in his life that had been less than pleasant. I was glad that he was done dealing with them. At times, my grief has been a rock. But if I concentrate, and dig deep, I am able to locate gratitude. And it is a pillow.

September 19, 2009

Your brothers and sister are wearing red today. I bet you are too. I am wearing my Mante shirt. In loving memory.

Family has always been a big deal to me. I like the huge celebrations and the tiniest of moments. I will dress everyone in the same color both to showcase and inspire our solidarity. One thing I wish more people understood is that Zumante is still part of our unit. His death won't rob us of that. He will always be included in the huge celebrations and the tiniest of moments. In loving memory.

September 20, 2009

A couple of years ago, I bought a book called Even If I Did Something Awful. You were having a pretty awful time trying to cope with life, and I thought the book was perfect, because it said that no matter what, we would have to solve our problems, and when all was said and done, I would still love you—even if you did something awful. Every time we read that book together, we both cried. Since you died, I have sometimes felt that you were testing that promise. You see, the thing you have done this time really is truly awful. And although you have probably done the most awful thing a child can do to a parent, I still love you. More than ever.

Being a mother is a hard job. Just like any other mom, I have butted heads with my children. I have thought some of their antics were just plain awful. It is probable that I will feel that way again. What I will also feel again is the unwavering assurance that nothing can alter the love I have for my kids. Even if they do something awful.

September 20, 2009

Maxie is sick. I am thinking of how you absolutely hated to see the other children not feeling well, how you always said it worried you. You were such an amazing big brother. I'm glad I had you first, glad that all of us were blessed enough to know you. Thank you.

From infancy, Zumante seemed wise beyond his years. He made my transition into motherhood easier. I marveled at the way he instinctively had characteristics that many people have to work at. What a special soul. Every child is.

September 20, 2009

I'm getting ready to look for a headstone for you. This all seems so dumb. What sense does it make that you should need a headstone?

I have, at times, sat and gazed upon my children in disbelief. It's hard to wrap my brain around the fact that I had something to do with their existence. Me? Someone's mom? Wow. Me? Looking at headstones because my child died? Truly unbelievable. I guess disbelief and denial are parts of grief too.

September 21, 2009

Missing you. Always. Remembering. Always. Hurting. Always.

If I am breathing, I am missing my son. When you are a mom, nothing can disturb your bond with your child. It is no less strong when your child leaves you to go to daycare or school; it remains firm in the face of time and distance. It is always intact. It is true that death kills. But it can't kill a mother's love.

September 22, 2009

There are so many emotions at war within me. A great deal of the time, I just have this ball of turmoil in my stomach. It scares me when I think of having your memories, but not you. I need for this to be different. I want to wake up from this horrid nightmare and I know I won't. It baffles me that it is possible to live with this much hurt. It seems as if my body should just collapse under the strain of trying to live. I'm not without you, but I am. You'll never leave me, but you're gone. And I can't even begin to comprehend it. Nothing makes any sense. I don't get why the sun still rises and shines or why the world still turns. My sun is neither rising nor setting. My world doesn't turn.

I have observed people observing me. I have overheard comments about how I still smile, and do what needs to be done. I don't blame people for not getting it. I don't get it either. But what I do get—what I understand very clearly—is that the world is never the same once your child dies.

September 23, 2009

There are times when I am having so many thoughts that I can't manage to have even one idea.

The death of my son has been overwhelming. I think a lot, but I have very little control over my thoughts. It's hard to focus on things requiring focus. The list of stages of grief is extensive. I can't recite it. But, for me, confusion is on the list.

September 23, 2009

Today your sister said that when she grows up and has a baby boy, she is going to name him Zumante. One of your brothers was praying for you to come back alive. Another is wondering if you have forgotten how to do the Jerk. And your baby brother asked me if I know where you are. I don't even have the solace of tears.

Things can happen which have the power to alter the entire course of your life. Things that were so important may cease to be important at all, and things that were never before considered may become top priorities. It can feel like a tidal wave has knocked you off of your feet. You may want to cry, but you just can't manage to. Everything has shifted. It's a shift I could do without.

September 23, 2009

Thinking of you. I'm so glad that you chose me to be your mom.

I think that perhaps before a spirit is born, it considers the possibilities. And for whatever reason, Zumante chose me. And God, in his infinite wisdom, agreed.

September 24, 2009

There are horribly painful times when it seems that you are just beyond my reach. I will turn a corner and sense that I have just missed you, or enter a room and think that you have just left it. It hurts. I am constantly looking for you in the places that you should be, and you are absent from them. Your bed lies empty, your television unwatched, and sometimes I just want to scream over the injustice of it all. You should be here, not only as a memory, but HERE, in the flesh. Here, laughing, and fighting with the other kids, and trying to get out of your homework, and eating up all of the food. I am tired—simply worn out from the sheer act of living without you also living. My head aches from trying to make sense of this. There is no sense in this. I never knew that I could love another person so much. I never knew I could hurt so badly. I wish I didn't have to know.

Emptiness is a part of grief. Longing and despair are parts of grief. I wish that I could skip them. But I have no control in this process. Death forces you to realize your limitations. Then you deal with them.

September 25, 2009

As always, I am thinking of you. Remembering all of the things we did as a family. The joy you had in your life. The joy you brought to so many lives. The joy you brought to my life. Some of it left with you.

It is crucial to be able to locate joy in your life. I hope and pray that remembering joy is an indication that it will come again.

September 25, 2009

Tonight your sister suggested that maybe you were given the wrong medicine in the hospital. I explained that the hospital did all they could. We talked about how you needed to have other medicine, long before the hospital. And she asked me, not for the first time, why you weren't just given what you needed. I told her that I don't know. It is such a challenge trying to explain what happened. I see your siblings struggle to understand. And I think, how could they possibly understand? I don't.

When someone you love dies, it is natural to search for a reasonable explanation. Generally, you can find something that, at least, partially satisfies. There may well be an explanation. It is a bit much to try to convince yourself that it is "reasonable." When your child dies, you feel like "reason" is dead too.

September 25, 2009

Earlier, I was reflecting about how you were so excited at the prospect of being ten. Wow. Double digits. Fifth grade. You were looking forward to so many things. You were going to get a cell phone (smile) and start drum lessons. You were going to build a portfolio and apply to a school of the arts. And your tenth birthday arrived and we had to sing happy birthday at the cemetery. Fifth grade started and your name was no longer on the roster. Your cell phone is a charm that I am saving. There will be no drum lessons. No portfolio. No arts school. And such a long list of other things that won't be happening. I am angry. And beyond sad. I think of all that you could have been and were going to be and I almost double over with the pain. And then I think of all that you were and all that you are and it gives me some strength. I am angry. And beyond sad. But I am also very clear about a couple of things. You did not have all of the life that I wished for. That is a tragedy. But what a life you did have. What a legacy you left. I am honored to be your mommy.

Death is a most despicable thief. It leaves you feeling robbed of moments and experiences. The trick is to remember all of the gifts that life has given. Some things cannot be stolen.

September 25, 2009

Sometimes when I think of you, I smile. Sometimes I think of you and cry. Sometimes I think of you and don't know what to do. So I do both.

Zumante died and I found myself on an emotional roller coaster. I am quite sure that I will be a lifetime passenger. Perhaps the hills will become less steep and frequent, perhaps the turbulence will lessen. Until then…

September 27, 2009

When I found out that I was pregnant with you, I was terrified. I thought, "Oh, crap! What have I done?!" It wasn't long though before I was ridiculously excited. I looked for the perfect little clothing, and the perfect little diaper bag. Titi Niecy threw a baby shower and I was just tickled. Every night, I rubbed my tummy, and sang to you, told you I loved you, and read you a book. I still have the first book you were ever given. It was Love You Forever. Imagine that.

Now that Zumante is gone, most people would think it's odd that I still mother him. It makes sense to me. I still search for the perfect. I try to keep pace with where he would be if he were alive. I'll love him forever. I'm his mommy forever.

September 27, 2009

In this moment, I can't begin to communicate where I am. How this hurts.

After a child dies, many emotions are present. Zumante's death hurt my feelings. It's hard to describe. I'm working on it.

September 27, 2009

Guess how much I love you?

I love Zumante with all of my being. I love him more than the depths are deep. The unit of measure does not exist that could define the love of a mother for her child.

September 28, 2009

Today I found a felt bunny that I made for you your first Easter. And a calendar where I wrote down so many of your firsts—the day you said your first word (it was baba, but you meant bye-bye—I could tell because you waved), how much you weighed at each doctor appointment, the first time you rolled over, your first tub bath, what you ate and enjoyed any given day. The first year and a half of your life, I was just your mommy, and I had nothing to focus on but you. I stayed home with you and never missed a thing. I had to be forced to be without you (just ask Titi Niecy). I eventually learned how to let you be outside of my range of vision, but not very far outside, and never for long. The pain I am in, thinking of how long it has been since I have heard your voice say "Mommy." The pain I am in, thinking of the fact that I am actually supposed to live an entire lifetime despite the fact that you have died. The pain I am in. The pain. The pain. thepainthepain-thepainthepainthepainthepainthepainthepain

I miss you.

There are times after your child dies that the entire world is composed of one thing, and that thing is pain. It is both sharp and dull, both hot and cold, both delicate and suffocating. It is hard and heavy. It is public and private, loud and quiet, relentless in its pursuit. It just is.

September 28, 2009

The last time you called me Mommy was July 16th. In your last moments before you lost consciousness, I held you in my arms. I cried even as I rocked you and told you it was okay. And you left me. How will it ever be okay?

Well, the truth is that it won't ever be "okay." But the truth is, also, that I am glad that it was Zumante and I in his last moments of consciousness. I am the last thing he really saw, the last thing he heard. My arms around him was the last thing he knew. I'm glad. Even though it will never be okay, there will always be things I can be glad about.

September 28, 2009

Today is a rough day. Like all the others since you died.

Two months after Zumante died, life was still rough. One year after Zumante died, life is still rough. I imagine that the rough will never completely disappear. I acknowledge and accept that, and do my best to deal with it.

September 30, 2009

I am not okay. It is interesting, the way people seem to think that I am doing well. I am sometimes functional. Sometimes not. But I am definitely not okay. I am screaming in my head, crying in my soul, aching from the top of my head to the tip of my toes. I don't know how to answer when I am confronted with "Hi. How are you?" I don't know how I am. I just am.

I wish I could convince people that grief and mourning are not only identified by how withdrawn one becomes. My sorrow is no less profound because I have maintained my ability to walk upright. Sometimes grief is invisible to the naked eye. It doesn't mean that it doesn't exist.

September 30, 2009

I am confused and probably confusing. I feel so bad about feeling bad. It is awful to try and get things done, or carry on in a "normal" fashion when my world lies shattered at my feet. Oh, how I wish things were different. My life hurts.

Since Zumante died, I have expended a considerable amount of energy wishing I could rewind the clock. It has been to no avail. I cannot change what has already happened. I can only go forward.

September 30, 2009

It feels as though I am being torn to shreds. I call for you and you don't answer me. I keep looking for you and I can't locate you. I have washed your clothes and I take them out for you and you don't wear them. I have told people that you died and I don't really believe it. I have been told (and I have told people) that I will make it but I don't believe that either. It is so hard to have courage. So hard to just keep doing what life requires of me. I am drowning. Your last words to me were "Mommy, I can't breathe anymore. It's too hard." And it is. I can't breathe either.

Zuton Lucero-Mills

Losing a child to death is more than a mental exercise. The physical ramifications are also very real. Grief is a terminal illness. I caught it July 20, 2009.

Through the storm...

When Zumante was born, I couldn't imagine leaving him in the care of anyone else. By the time he was four and ready to begin preschool, the two of us were firmly attached to each other. His first day of school, I gave him a hug and dropped him off with apprehension. I trudged from the building and paused outside of his classroom. Peeking in the window, I discovered Mante happily engaged in play. I cried. The idea that he could be away from me and still be perfectly fine made me both happy and sad. It meant that he really was autonomous. What a concept!

We (or maybe I should say I) made it through ECE that year. I instantly fell in love with the teacher. Kindergarten, and each following grade, brought greater joy. The school was an amazing place with amazing people and it felt like home. My children were educated and nurtured and I was welcomed and embraced. The school relationship was, and remains, cherished.

During Zumante's hospital stay and after his death, several calls were made directly to teachers. There were school wide notifications. I spoke with the teachers, who spoke

with each other, and they, in turn, contacted Zumante's classmates.

I recall answering a knock at my front door after Zumante died. The school secretary was standing there and she put her arms around me without a word. That set the tone for what followed.

Some of that time period is still a blur to me. There is, however, a great deal that I remember with amazing clarity. I know that my family was watched over and cared for in those initial, heartwrenching days. The funeral was filled with our school family. Zumante's 4th grade (and final) teacher spoke beautifully. My soul was uplifted.

The day that school started in the fall was horrendous for me. I walked into the building trembling, painfully aware of my son's absence. I thought I was going to have a nervous breakdown. The school staff walked me through what needed to be done. They firmly reassured me that I could lean on them and that my children—including Zumante—were in a good place. The next day, and the next week, and the next month, I relied heavily on them. Their patience was unwavering.

It made life so much easier to not have to worry excessively about my children when I left them at school. From the classroom to the principal's office, they were enveloped in love.

It was not only our fragile spirits that were sustained. At least three times a week, either my school or the children's saw to it that dinner was provided for us. We were so grateful. It reminded us to eat, and removed the pressure of having to focus long enough to prepare a meal.

Shortly after school had resumed, I received a phone call from the school resource advocate. In a voice filled with emotion, she explained to me that the school was building a garden on the property. It would have a variety of things planted in it and there were local organizations that had committed to help. I thought that it all sounded very nice, but I remember wondering briefly why she was contacting me about it. Then I found out. "Zuton," she said. "We want to dedicate it to Zumante."

It was a gesture that I had not anticipated. Not only does the garden provide a new place and way for students to learn, it is a living reminder of my son. It even contains a plaque with his picture. It says to me that his school will remember and honor him.

At the close of the school year, I attended the 5th grade continuation. I scanned the auditorium, full of my son's friends. My hands were shaking and my heart was pounding. I'd had conversations about Zumante being awarded a continuation certificate and I sat in my seat with my emotions fluctuating wildly. I had a hard time controlling my breathing. It was so important to me to have Zumante recognized. I appreciate that the school understood. They have been, and continue to be, remarkable.

This garden is dedicated
in memory of
ZUMANTE LUCERO

Congratulations!

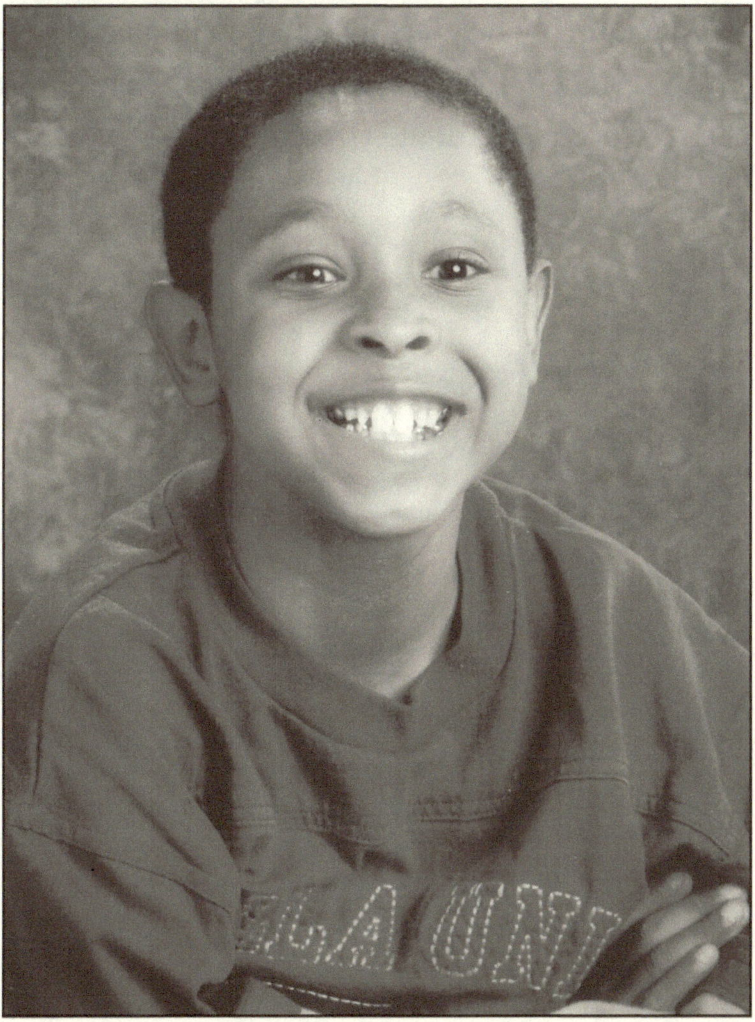

October 1, 2009

I spent a great deal of the day crying and calling your name. I stared at nothing a lot. I wondered. I lamented. I shook my head as though I could just shake it all away. I sighed. I heaved. I yelled. I sat silent. I worried. I gazed at the sky. I questioned. I missed you.

On any given day after the death of a child, the full spectrum of emotions can be experienced. It is not unusual to laugh and cry, smile and scream, all in the space of a heartbeat. I know that sounds extreme. That's because it is.

October 3, 2009

As I walked across the lawn today, I recalled how I paced the yard with you in my arms after you lost consciousness. It was the last time I physically carried you. Now I carry you in my heart.

Mere hours before Zumante's asthma attack, we were on a field trip. I carried him piggyback style and he rested his head against me. I hadn't carried him like that in a long time. I'm glad I did that day. Who knew that there wouldn't be another chance?

October 7, 2009

I miss you from head to toe. It has caused my hair to become brittle and my migraines to be frequent. My eyes grow tired quickly and there is a roaring in my ears. My chest hurts. My stomach is tied in knots. My legs feel wobbly, and my feet often don't want to carry me. I am faint. My appetite fails me. Sleep sometimes escapes me. I have an awful time getting up in the morning. I have constant anxiety—and that, I think, is the most ridiculous of all. Anxiety for what? The worst that could happen already has.

Grief is a war that ravages the entire body. The entire self is battered, and aching, and scarred. The ligaments are torn, the bones fractured. And there is still so much anxiety. I think it comes from somehow knowing that your broken body will never make it out of the war zone.

October 15, 2009

It has been awhile since I have added text to this page. It is not because I have not been thinking of you. I think of you with every breath I take—and all of the time in between.

When your child has died, you are consumed with thoughts of them. There is no forgetting—even for a split second. Sometimes, people think differently, but they are wrong.

October 15, 2009

There are times when I am literally lost or just generally confused. I have made wrong turns on roads that I travel every day. Nothing is familiar to me. Nothing makes sense. I wonder if this is what the rest of my life will be—if I will remain forever lost; always wandering in search of that one thing that eludes me. It makes me ache. I need you. And I know that no matter how much I need you, it won't return you to me. I won't wake up with the realization that I simply had a ridiculous nightmare. I get frustrated and aggravated sometimes when someone who means well reminds me that you "will always be in our hearts." Perhaps, for some, the heart is a sufficient place for you to be. However, for me, it is not sufficient. It pisses me off to only get to have you in my heart. I want you by my side. At the dinner table. In your classroom. Giving me a hug. And I can't have any of that. No wonder I can't find my way home.

When life is as it should be, home is a safe haven. It is where one can go to "just get away from it all." It is a cocoon. A place to relax. You can always go home… Except that, after the death of your child, it's hard to recall just where home is. Which way to go to get there. What exactly it looks like. It's baffling to think of home. It used to be wherever your child was.

October 15, 2009

I was driving today when the realization that you are dead struck me like a jolt of lightning. This often happens. And then I will feel a heavy, suffocating grief. And my heart will pound and I am overwhelmed by the fear that all of this is real.

It can be horrendous to think of your life as being real. It can be helpful, then, to allow oneself the indulgence of believing it is not real. Of course, the problem with this is that it <u>is</u> real, and you really can't help it.

October 15, 2009

Death terrifies me. I alternate between the fear that other loved ones will die, and the fear that I will die and my loved ones will feel as I do now. I am glad that you don't have to know fear anymore. I just wish there had been another way.

Life is scary. When death has become your immediate life, it is horrific. When I am able to still my shaking, I know that Zumante is free of fear. If one of us must be afraid, I prefer that it be me.

October 15, 2009

I have always been teased about being an eternal optimist. I am used to being known as someone who smiles abundantly, and can find the silver lining in any cloud. It is a challenge to be that person these days. I looked for the positives when you were in the hospital. I believed not only in the possibility that you would recover, I was absolutely sure that you would. I was firm in my belief. I didn't waver. I didn't entertain the thought that you would die. And when I realized that you would, I was crushed. Devastated. Blindsided. And bewildered. I have always known that things generally happen the way they are supposed to. Things work out the way that they are meant. Yet this is different. It is not possible that this is how it was supposed to happen, that this is how it is meant to be. I have to question whether I have been wrong my entire life. And I ask myself, in weak moments, the point of being an optimist. I believed in the power of positivity when it mattered the most—and it failed me.

I am still an optimist. It hurts like hell, but I still know that things generally happen the way that they are supposed to. In the darkest moment, a light can be found if you search hard enough. It is true that I have thrown up my hands and said "Just forget it!" But I can't. I haven't been wrong my entire life. The power of positivity helps me put one foot in front of the other.

October 15, 2009

There is a massive amount of chaos in my head. It makes me feel rather frantic. Physical chaos in my life causes me to panic. I am desperately trying to bring order to my life. And even as I attempt to organize the clutter, I know, in quiet despair, that it can't happen. The order has been disrupted. Things could be perfect externally, and the clutter in my head would not clear. I know that with absolute certainty. It makes it hard to hope.

After Zumante died, I was often fidgety. I needed things to be done in their proper order. One thing that death makes uncomfortably clear is that we cannot control everything. Being human, we try to prove the opposite. The best way is to find things that we actually can control.

October 15, 2009

When I am trying not to listen, I will hear the other kids. They pick wish flowers or gaze up at the stars and wish for you to come back. And even though no one can hear me, I am wishing too.

All of the children I know make wishes. They think that if they do it a certain way, their wish will come true. Most adults would never admit it, but we make wishes even more than children do. We even expect some of them to come true.

October 16, 2009

I discovered right away that it doesn't work to take things day by day. Days are much too large and unmanageable. When viewed as a whole, my days are consistently hard or harder. I take it moment by moment instead. When I have a difficult moment, I try to just breathe and wait for a less painful moment to arrive. The breathing itself brings pain. I remember that it was breathing that was so hard for you. It is what took you away. People take breathing for granted. Early in your life, you became conscious of every breath. During your life, I, too, was conscious of your every breath. With your death, I became conscious of mine. It hurts that I am breathing and you aren't.

In life, so many things are taken for granted. Zumante's death caused me to examine, more so than ever before, that breathing should not be taken for granted. Nothing should.

October 17, 2009

It's just not right. I was looking at your name heading this memorial page, and the wrongness of it all was enough to bring me to my knees. It's not right. God got it wrong this time.

Zuton Lucero-Mills

The harsh reality is that there is a lot of wrong in the world. Zumante's story includes a significant amount of wrong. But right or wrong, it is what it is. I have no choice but to wait for God's explanation.

October 17, 2009

Sometimes my grief is a raging storm, carrying me away with the downpouring of tears. The world is gray and tumultuous, and the sky is shattered by the lightning of my misery. The ground is flooded and I drown even as I struggle to find my way to dry land. I choke and spit and gasp and flail, but I have forgotten how to swim and mere floating doesn't seem to be an option. There is no shelter. The wind of my confusion howls in my ears. And yet. Yet, I get up in the morning and get people dressed and take them to school. I go to work and pretend that I am making it. I'm not.

I have become an award-winning actress. I may be the only one aware of it, but my life is now a stage. I spend every second performing as though my life depends on it. Maybe it does. If I can sustain my act long enough, maybe it will one day feel real.

October 17, 2009

Sometimes my grief is a quiet despair. It leaves me without the solace of my tears. I have nothing except the stark emptiness that comes from knowing that my child is dead. I can't fix it. I feel like I should have been able to keep you alive just by sheer will and by virtue of being your mother. You were—you are—my Mante. My only Mante. I begged you and begged God to not take my Mante away. Do you remember? My cries went unheeded and I lost part of myself. At the cemetery, the minister mistakenly said my name instead of yours and I knew it was no mistake. God took me when he took you. No matter what joy I have in store for the rest of my life, I would trade it to have you back. I don't know how to live without you living also.

Living is a skill that I once had that I have lost. I forgot how to live in much the same manner as other skills are forgotten when not used properly. Little by little, I am attempting to relearn. There doesn't appear to be an alternative.

October 17, 2009

Today I kept thinking that your brothers were you. And every time I realized that they weren't you, I felt like I was being choked. The lessons that I learned from you are at completely opposite ends of the spectrum. Before you were born, I never knew how deeply I could love. And when you died, it taught me how deeply I could hurt. It astounds me that I can be this broken and still survive.

Zuton Lucero-Mills

I have been so deeply wounded that it astounds me that it's not more physically evident. It strikes me as odd that the blood is not pouring from me. I'm amazed to be alive. When you are living in grief, you cannot fathom how it is possible.

October 17, 2009

When I cry, your baby brother asks me if I am okay. I look at his little face, so like yours, and I cry more. I think of how you were so perfect as a big brother, and how much you are missed. We were lucky to have you.

There was a point at which, on a daily basis, one of my children would find me crying. I cried for Zumante, who had gone on, but I cried also for the rest of us, who had been left behind. Zumante is so missed. I don't expect missing him to pass away.

October 17, 2009

I don't think its strength that keeps me functioning. I think it's dumb luck.

People that I think know me well, and people that don't really know me at all, have something in common. There are those on both sides who are of the opinion that I am strong. I don't think so. It certainly doesn't feel that way.

October 17, 2009

I think that you were amazing and special. Talented and creative. Thoughtful and sincere. Sympathetic and caring. Wise. Smart. Funny. Articulate. Spirited. Genuine. Kind. Unique. Understanding. Patient. Giving. Loving. The world is less without you in it.

Zuton Lucero-Mills

One thing that can be quickly discovered about a child is how awesome they are. Kids are huge gifts in tiny packaging. They can fairly bubble over with their awesomeness. The world seems fuller somehow. Upon the death of a child, the world is somehow diminished.

October 17, 2009

My life feels like one big conflict. How can I be expected to do or be much of anything right now? But I can't stop doing or being either. I can't function well enough to satisfy basic life requirements. I can only function well enough to ache. I can do that with amazing proficiency.

I feel inadequate with alarming frequency. It can be difficult, at best, to carry on. I have had to keep telling myself that the world will not end if I don't keep up a Superwoman act. And really, if it did end, how much would I care?

October 20, 2009

Within an hour after you died, the very world seemed to shift. There were tornadoes and hailstorms. People were baffled. All of this going on in Denver, in the middle of summer, and the middle of the night? The probability was near nothing. But when your spirit exited your body, something mighty occurred. I think that you ran and yelled, overcome with the feeling of being free. I believe that God and the angels rejoiced, and their combined voices appeared to us on earth as lightning and thunder. I believe that the ancestors danced and sang and the result was tornadoes and balls of ice. I understood what was happening. It made sense to me. But very few things do.

Each of us, I think, must have something to believe in and hold onto. I believe in God. I believe in heaven. I believe wholly and deeply in a number of things. It lends me a measure of sanity in this insane time.

October 22, 2009

Yesterday when I awoke, it was snowing. My stomach clenched and my heart raced. Even though I know that it is only your body in the ground, the thought of any part of you being cold pains me. I wanted to get a blanket and take it to your grave. It hurts, knowing that your body is buried and the earth will freeze around you. When I first saw you in the casket, there was glass covering you, and I panicked for a moment, thinking that you couldn't breathe. Then I realized that you had already stopped breathing and I just collapsed. I miss you.

Zuton Lucero-Mills

I am not always rational. I don't share a great deal of what goes on in my head for fear of sounding like a lunatic. Then again, I can't expect everything to make sense to everyone. I have not lost my mind…but I have lost my son.

October 23, 2009

Your absence is a huge gaping hole in my life. It is never outside of my realm of consciousness. Instead, I am confronted with the reality of it every moment. I open my eyes in the morning and my first thought is of you. I get the other children ready for school and swallow back the tears long enough to do what needs to be done. Sometimes, I can't swallow them back. So I cry. I call their names out loud, and scream your name silently. I am broken. Battered. I think sometimes that God must be watching me struggle and questioning his own judgment. I am so so afraid that all of this is real. I am dismayed that all of this is real. I am enraged that all of this is real. I am confused about how all of this could be real. It makes me sick to my stomach.

For most of my life, I have been in generally good health. I have seldom been ill. But since Zumante died, that has changed. I didn't get the connection initially, but there most certainly is one. I have had a stomachache 98% of the time for the last year. Any angel-mom will tell you that this is not unique. Grief makes you sick.

October 23, 2009

There are many times when I am in such severe pain that I am literally paralyzed. And times when I get short of breath as I remember your shortness of breath that last Thursday. And times when I feel faint, recalling the moment that you fainted. And times when I am panicking and crying as you did. Times when I am fighting as you did. I feel like I am dying as you did.

Part of being a mother is sharing the pain of your child. You want to soothe away every hurt. Unfortunately, death is a hurt that even the best mother cannot soothe away.

October 23, 2009

I miss you. I have made concentrated efforts to think of something happy and it is overshadowed by my longing for you. Like tonight. We had fun and you weren't here. Some fun.

I have always been fun loving. Now, even in the midst of my joy, there is sorrow. I have learned how to smile with my mouth even when I can't make the smile reach my eyes. Eventually, maybe it will.

October 23, 2009

I feel as though my very personality has been altered. I'm not who I once was. I don't even remember who I once was—except that I was much closer to whole. I had you.

Things are different now. It is not my imagination. There exists a defining moment. There was life before Zumante died, and there is a pale imitation of life since then. Who I am can never again be who I was.

October 23, 2009

You are my Mante,
My only Mante.
You make me happy—
When skies are grey.
You'll never know, son,
How much I love you.
Why'd you take my Mante away?

When Zumante was an infant, I enjoyed singing to him. I would take a song and personalize it for him. The Sunshine Song, which I changed to "The Mante Song," was one of the earliest I sang to him. It was also the last.

October 23, 2009

I am trying to keep this in perspective. I should probably be confident that God knows what he is doing. On the contrary, I'm quite upset with God. How can he be satisfied with what he's done?

I was not taught that it is wrong to question God. On the contrary, I was taught that it is okay to question, that doing so helps you to grow. I don't worry that being upset and questioning God will lead to my being punished. I'm pretty sure God can take it. I imagine that he cries not only for me, but also with me.

October 23, 2009

This is a struggle. I can't make up my mind. I rage at God and everything else and then I remind myself. You are safe now. You are secure now. You are happy now. You are healthy now. You are okay now. But I am not. No one else is. Is it selfish of me to keep thinking of what the rest of us are going through? And I wonder also. I did my best to keep you safe. I tried to provide you with security. Weren't you happy? As okay as you could be? And I worked so hard to keep you healthy. I did my best. And you died anyway. I don't understand the lesson here.

When bad things happen, we tell ourselves that there is a lesson to be learned. I have learned some harsh lessons. I have also learned that I am not done learning.

October 23, 2009

I am not trying to be strong. I have given myself, and all of those around me, permission to not be strong. I recognize that my feelings are valid, and I am allowed to honor them. I am not going to try to feel something other than what I am feeling. I am mad. I am devastated. I am confused. I am heartbroken. I am conflicted. I am in pain. I am distressed. I am lonely. I am. And all of what I am is okay with me whether or not it is okay with anyone else. You are MY son. I will do this MY way.

It never occurred to me that I would face something so horribly awful. The problem with sympathy is that it is seldom far-reaching enough. People tend to have preconceived notions about what grieving looks like. I'm here to challenge those notions. I hope I don't do it alone.

October 26, 2009

Last night I dreamed that you died. And then lived. And then died again. I held you. And even as you died, I was so grateful to be seeing you. I felt so blessed at the opportunity to hug you and talk to you. I hated watching you die all over again. I loved seeing you again. I miss you so much. Can you come to my dreams and just live for one night?

It is sweet agony to be visited in sleep by the child who you know is dead when you are awake. Even though it's desired, you almost can't stand it when it happens. I used to pray fervently to see Zumante in my dreams. But it makes waking up harder than usual.

October 26, 2009

You and I used to talk a lot about being grateful. Very early on, you grasped the concept. And even though you sometimes had a momentary lapse, you were pretty good about being grateful. That impressed me. It impresses me even more so now. I have a great deal to be grateful for, but it is a bit of a challenge. I can't have the one thing I desperately need. It is not easy to be grateful and miserable at the same time. Mommy loves you.

I am constantly performing a delicate balancing act. I balance work and home, thoughts and feelings, obligations with ability. I am not always successful. Things get dropped. I pick them up and balance again.

October 26, 2009

I feel so fragmented. Nothing in my life flows effortlessly these days. I recall things as snapshots instead of complete stories. You called for me. Snap. You passed out. Snap. In the emergency room. Snap. Down for two minutes. Snap. Six minutes. Snap. Days in the ICU. Snap. You died. Snap.

Now that I think about it, of course I only see snapshots. My heart can't stand replaying the complete story.

My memory is incomplete. When you are traumatized, the body naturally tries to protect itself. Shutting down can be one method of protection—another is shutting things out. It is important to remember that there is no shame in admitting that you are having a hard time. When life fragments, tape it together.

October 26, 2009

I don't want to do this. I hurt so much. I miss you so much. I would give anything.

I have things that are precious to me. If there were the slightest chance that I could relinquish them and regain Zumante, I wouldn't hesitate. But death is not flexible. There are no bargains to be made. There is nothing that can be given to conquer death. Instead, I plan to give my everything to conquer life.

October 27, 2009

Halloween is coming. I feel as though someone has already played a mean trick on me.

I have seen comedians tell jokes that didn't earn a single laugh. It is not the timing or the presentation. It is that the joke itself is just not funny. I have known of children's pranks that didn't cause me to smile. In witnessing those types of scenarios, I have sometimes cringed, but I didn't carry the burden with me. Death is not shrugged off so easily.

October 28, 2009

Today was hard. I wish you could have turned ten.

The timing of Zumante's death has haunted me. It was ten days before his brother turned two and three weeks before he would have been ten. The timing was not good—but there never is a good time.

October 30, 2009

This is not getting easier. It is getting harder.

I'm not sure why people think there is a timeline for grief. Somehow, there is the expectation that a particular course will be followed. This is a myth. There is no roadmap. Sometimes it gets harder instead of easier. Sometimes, the way is rougher instead of smoother.

October 30, 2009

For the last several minutes, I have sat and stared at this blank page. I have nothing to give. My ears are roaring again and I am shivering from a cold that is coming from the inside. I am suffering. I wonder what I am being punished for. I miss your presence at the dinner table, miss your contributions to all of our lives. For a while now, I have simply been in too much pain to write anything substantial here. The other day, I cried all the way home because a song came on the radio. The singer was lamenting his love lost, wishing he could get a do over, insisting that she was his very air and he couldn't survive without her. I can relate. Except that I have no chance of a do over. It is done. Over.

Journaling in this way is something I have needed. At times, the words fairly pour from my soul. But not always. Sometimes, the pain is so deep, I can't find the words to express it. This is one of those times. I know that, eventually, this too shall pass.

October 30, 2009

I know that you are in more capable hands than mine. I have told people as much. Yet, I do not always find this comforting. Sometimes, I find it maddening.

The idea that someone else could take better care of your child is a tough pill to swallow. Even though Zumante is in the care of God himself, I hate the idea that I could be outdone. He may be God—but I am MOM.

October 30, 2009

I was looking forward to the future. If I had known, I wouldn't have.

It is natural to look forward to things. Anticipation brings added excitement to life. I never learned to anticipate the negative. If I had, I would likely dread the future. Even now, I'm not willing to do that.

October 30, 2009

People have told me, on several occasions, that they wouldn't be functional if it was their child. They tell me that I am strong. That they don't know how I do it. I have heard so many versions of this that they all run together like one big, unintelligible train. I don't think they get it. I have somehow fooled them. I am not functioning. I am not strong. I have come undone. I am lying on the floor in a million pieces. I am not doing "well". I am a woman whose child died. A woman who heard her son's last words and tried to comfort him when there was no comfort. A woman who had to tell a roomful of children that their brother was going to die. A woman who had to have her son removed from a ventilator. A woman who felt her son's last heartbeat. A woman who wrote her son's obituary and planned his funeral. A woman who celebrated a tenth birthday at a cemetery. I am not fine. I don't even entertain the possibility.

A mother's grief can be incomprehensible unless you too are a grieving mother. Writing this book is my attempt to shed some light. Perhaps I will not bring full sunshine, but maybe the break of dawn…

October 30, 2009

I have come to despise waking up in the morning. It is always the same. Before I open my eyes, I have the crushing, horrid realization that nothing has changed overnight. By the time I force my eyes open, my stomach is churning and my head is pounding. I am shaking. I am shaken. I search the far recesses of my mind for some indication that I am capable of making it through the next few moments. There is no such indication. So I wait. And ponder. I finally rise, spent, and I wonder what to do with myself. I do a lot of wondering. But I never get any answers. I walk around the house in a fog. I look for you. I look for me. Both of us remain lost.

It takes so much effort for me to get out of bed in the morning that, by the time I do, I am spent. Exhausted. I must be guided by a higher power, because my own power is terribly inconsistent.

Through the storm...

The pain of losing Zumante has been, and continues to be, profound. In the midst of the pain, though, my family and I have been blessed with tremendous support. During Zumante's time in the hospital, there was a steady stream of visitors. The waiting room was filled. Children drew pictures to hang in his room. School personnel, extended family, and friends were all present. In Zumante's final moments, he was not alone—and neither was I.

The news of Zumante's passing spread rapidly. We received countless calls and cards expressing condolences. My children were well cared for while arrangements were made and the offers of help were seemingly endless. I knew that Zumante was loved while he was living, and the display of love after his death moves me deeply. I would not have made it otherwise.

There are so many beautiful stories of others' kindness to my family. Even after so much time has passed, my family still recalls all that was done for us. In a world where we so often take notice of the negative, the positive was simply astounding.

Zumante's death ripped me to shreds. Those around me were ointments for my wounds. They were living bandages and stitches. Words and hugs, prayers and deeds nurtured me. Even while I lamented the heartlessness of a world that would strip a mother of her son, I recognized the numerous hearts that would not have allowed me to fend for myself.

There is so much power in kindness. Kindness gave me strength. Kindness gave me hope. I want to be sure to pass it on.

November 2, 2009

There are times when I become aware that my distress must be showing on my face. I can tell because, inevitably, someone will ask "What's wrong?" and I want to reply "What's right?"

I'm never quite sure how to answer. I don't want to lie. The truth is too involved. This is why there is an uncomfortable silence. I'm not trying to be rude. I'm just stumped.

November 4, 2009

It is an effort to be pleasant with a broken heart and a battered spirit. I don't think anyone knows exactly how much I put into forcing one foot in front of the other and pasting a smile across my face. It is exhausting. I want to just crawl into bed and pull the covers over my head. I don't want to face anyone or anything. I am painfully aware that this is not working. I have been wading through a pool of quicksand and I sink more every moment. I miss you.

I think that if my soul were bared for all to see, women would faint and men would burst into tears. I realize that it wasn't just yesterday that my son died. Please pardon me if I still feel like it was.

November 5, 2009

Sleep escaped me last night. At times, I tossed and turned trying to escape the troubling images. Other times, I lay still, resigned, knowing that there will never be an escape. I was relieved when the alarm went off. My relief lasted the space of a heartbeat. Now my heart is thumping painfully, and there is a bad taste in my mouth. Another day without you. I feel weak. I have always heard, and mostly believed, that God is a merciful God. Where is the mercy?

I know that mercy is present, but I can be hard pressed to recognize it. I try to remind myself that things can take different forms than we wish or expect. God's mercy is no exception.

November 7, 2009

"If ye have faith, as a grain of mustard seed..." It has always been my favorite scripture. I have lived by it. Faith is something that I have prided myself on having in abundance. I quoted it to you in the hospital. I still don't know if faith failed me, or if I simply had faith in the wrong way. I have been questioning so many things. The other day, I was puzzling over mercy. I am still not sure. I know that there was mercy for you.

There are so many puzzling things about life. I thought I had some of the answers, and when Zumante died I realized I don't even have all of the questions.

November 7, 2009

Today, I question faith. I am afraid to have it.

Having faith has become scary. I don't want it to be misplaced. I don't want to feel like it is futile. Then again, I don't think it's possible to make it without it.

November 7, 2009

The other day, I saw a flyer for basketball tryouts. Last year, you missed tryouts and you were so disappointed. You weren't going to miss it this year. But you did.

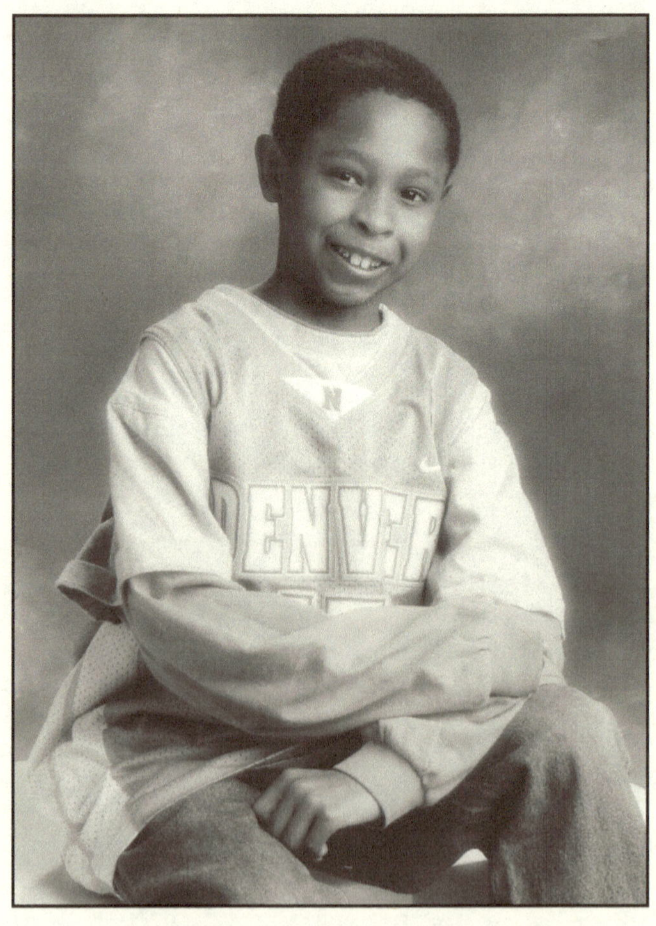

Zuton Lucero-Mills

Inasmuch as I lament the fact that Zumante is not doing the things he was before, I also lament the things he didn't have a chance to do. Basketball was one of many things that he was looking forward to in the very near future. I have learned that the future is not necessarily what we anticipate it to be.

November 7, 2009

My dance crew boys have been practicing the Jerk. Yesterday, as I watched them, I thought of how much you practiced that same dance. I miss your dancing feet. Your laugh. Your drawings. Your hugs. You.

Zumante did things with great gusto. It was infectious. I would want to dance because he looked like he was having such a fantastic time. I would laugh because his laugh was like an invitation. I miss Zumante for his sake. And I miss him for mine.

November 7, 2009

I feel so robbed. I started to talk to the children at school about the concept of thanksgiving and I had to change the subject. I don't feel very thankful. I think of you not struggling to breathe, and running and playing with wild abandon now, and I should be thankful. But I'm not. Why couldn't you have had that here?

Sometimes, I feel terribly bitter. I struggle against the sensation, but I am not always successful. It's a tall order to remember what to be thankful for. But these are my feelings. They are valid. I can own them.

November 7, 2009

The last couple of days, the pain of missing you has manifested itself as a horrible pain in my chest. I am afraid of a life like this—a life with you being separate from me. It's not right. Nothing is right anymore.

I try not to ponder life too much. It scares me. It is bad enough that Zumante isn't with me today. I cannot fathom this separation lasting the space of a lifetime. Things would be wrong even if they were perfect.

November 9, 2009

I cried a lot for you today. Some of my cries were of the silent, invisible variety. Other cries were great, gushing sobs, threatening to choke me with their force. None of my cries brought you home. And I know, even as I fight my knowing, that my cries cannot return you to me. I'm going to keep trying anyway. You're my favorite Mante.

It doesn't feel like it in the moment, but tears have healing power. I have cried to the point of utter exhaustion, and the circumstances of my life have been unchanged. But, sometimes, crying is all you can do. Sometimes the act of crying maintains your sanity.

November 11, 2009

I had nightmares last night. I woke, as usual, with a headache and a stomachache. Last night, the kids were playing and laughing wildly. As they laughed in one room, I cried in another. Their laughs cut through me like a sword because your laugh was missing from the chorus. It troubled me deeply. All things do.

There are so many things to be troubled about in this world. I didn't think so before. I never saw the point in being troubled over things I have no control over. Things have changed somewhat. I have nightmares and cry regularly. I am troubled regularly. And I regularly attempt to do something about it.

November 13, 2009

I encounter you in everything and everyone. This morning, as soon as I got to work, one of the kids shouted to me, “Guess what? I made the basketball team!” He was so proud, and I thought about how I expected to hear you say those same words this year. Last week, a child approached me to show off his turtle, and it reminded me of you and Squirt. My head aches and throbs with missing you. My heart breaks with missing you. Not every day. Every minute. Every second.

Zumante exists in every corner of my world. It is simultaneously gratifying and agonizing. It is no accident that Zumante seems woven into the entire world. He had a full life. We shared so many experiences. It makes perfect sense to be constantly reminded of him. It makes me smile and it makes me cry. I love that I have my memories. I wish there had been time to create more.

November 13, 2009

Today at school, they served fish sticks for lunch. I could smell it in the air, and my chest became tight. I knew it was enough to cause you to have an asthma attack. I was so glad that you are beyond that. Yet, at the same time, the thought that you are beyond that slammed into me with the force of a sledgehammer. I'm not sure if anyone noticed when I went to my knees to blink back the tears. I can't believe I have any left.

Grief can be both inconvenient and inconsiderate. It refuses to be confined to my home and has no regular hours. Grief is not acquainted with decorum and has no sense of practicality. When you are grieving, you are constantly in danger of being attacked by emotion. It strikes during breakfast. In the grocery store. On the highway. At work. At times, it appears as though the entire world is witnessing the breakdown. Other times, it is just you—on your knees—and no one really notices.

November 15, 2009

When I don't write here, I feel like I am neglecting you. I worry that you think I have forgotten. But I haven't. I thought of you as I dreamed, and you were my first thought when I woke. I think of you with each footstep, with each breath, with each heartbeat. I think of you every time I swallow, and every time I blink. I think of you when I smile and when I cry, when I am with others, and when I am alone. I think of you, and pray for you. I hope for you, and wish for you. I search for you. I yearn for you. I miss you.

When your child dies, the mother-child relationship does not. I still feel a need to care for Zumante. I must have a way to still do for him. So, I nurture his spirit. It means that I am still necessary. I still have a purpose. I am still Mante's mommy.

November 15, 2009

We visited your grave the other day. It hurt my feelings.

Denial can be a huge component of grief. Sometimes pretending gets me through a day. Having to face and deal with reality is crushing. The existence of a grave suggests that there has been a burial. A burial is the result of life leaving a body. When I see my son's grave, it is a confrontation. Me against reality. It hurts to lose.

November 15, 2009

I remember carrying you on my back that last Thursday. You put your arms around my neck and I was surprised that I could still carry you that way. You didn't feel like a burden. I was glad I could do it. I wish I could do it again.

Zuton Lucero-Mills

When I think of carrying Zumante, it reminds me of footprints. I carried him, and God carries us both. I find it comforting.

November 15, 2009

Watching your son die is like watching the world end. The trees and flowers wilt, the lakes and rivers dry out, the happy animal sounds vanish, and a nothingness overtakes the land. Finally, the sun sets, and all around is darkness. And you know that everything is forever changed. And your son is dead, so you don't really care. What good is any of it anyway?

There are moments when I loathe being in the world. It seems like a moot point. I try to remind myself that I have work to do. I try to force myself to care. I think that maybe if I force it long enough, maybe one day it will come naturally again.

November 16, 2009

I am a wreck. Today my grief is a raw, open wound. Acid flows across it as I attempt to make it through this day. I am so terribly tired. I have been searching for words to convey what I am going through and I can't. This devastation is all encompassing. I believed that it was final, but it isn't. It is ever evolving. Each time I think that I could not possibly feel worse, I do.

People try to be encouraging. They tell you that it will get easier as time passes. For me, a little over a year has passed. Nothing has changed. I acknowledge that this does not mean that I have been lied to. Time is a relative term. I won't make a judgment just yet.

November 22, 2009

It has been four months since you died. It is like a bad movie that is on constant replay in my head. I realize that you only died once, but as a result I die countless times a day. Your death eats at me. I haven't written here in days because my spirit has been paralyzed and even my fingers are affected. I miss you so much. There are so many thoughts swirling in my head, and I can't get them to flow through to this page. The paralysis is taking over again.

I have said that time is relative. It is also an odd, changeable creature. While it feels like an eternity since the death of Zumante, it simultaneously feels like it just happened moments ago. I feel like I have been hurting forever, yet the grief is very fresh and new. Overwhelming is an understatement.

November 24, 2009

I was in the car heading west the other day, and I noticed the mountains. They were snow-covered and the sky was a perfect blue backdrop. There were puffy white clouds in the sky and small birds flew in the distance. It was beautiful. I was struck by the beauty of it all. I felt like I was being mocked. It bothered me that God had the audacity to take you away and go on placing beauty in the world as though it still belonged. I was amazed that my eyes even had the capability to notice color. I notice only for short spans of time though. Before I had finished my drive, the snow-covered mountains looked ominous, and the blue sky seemed sad. The shapes of the clouds were strange and confusing and the song of the birds was painful to my ears. It was ugly. I was struck by the desolation of it all. I felt that my vision had cleared and I saw before me the world the way it has become for me.

When death touches your life, the whole of it is affected. Nothing is untouched or unchanged. Reality is altered. It is not simply the imagination running wild. Things do not just appear different. They actually are.

November 26, 2009

So it is Thanksgiving. I hurt so much. I am alternating between cooking, cleaning, and crying. Preparing the banana pudding, I thought of how your eyes lit up every time I made it. I want to scream. To run and keep on running until I reach the place where you are. I am desperately trying to give thanks. I AM thankful. I am thankful that I am your mom. I am thankful for all of your siblings. I am thankful for the love and support of family and friends. I am thankful for the kindness of strangers. I am thankful for a wonderful job. I am thankful for a home. I am thankful for food, clothing, and a vehicle. I am thankful for so many things, and in the midst of that, I still hurt so badly that I can barely breathe. I am thankful that I had your physical presence for almost ten years. I am thankful for all that I was able to give to you and share with you. I am thankful for the abundance that you gave and shared with me. I am thankful that you are not in pain today. I am thankful that you don't itch today. I am thankful that you can breathe freely today. I am thankful that you can run and play today. I am thankful that I can feel you around me today. I am thankful. But I am in agony.

What a complicated thing grief is. In viewing the world, you are confronted with a great many positive things. Often, it is hard to identify them. Sometimes, it is a challenge to acknowledge them. But it is more than just knowing and acknowledging. It is the other. The feeling that can't be shaken. Positive abounds. But still…

November 27, 2009

I miss you immensely.

I have discovered that some things change and some things don't. When your child dies, so much changes. But missing them doesn't. That is a constant.

November 28, 2009

My first major holiday without you. My mind raced in a million directions and many of my thoughts were jumbled. One thing made sense to me. You missed Thanksgiving. And I missed you.

Death causes many fragments. One of the most noticeable is time. Each hour, each day, it is apparent. But holidays can be especially fragmented and brutal. The consolation is that they pass.

November 29, 2009

The Eagles just won the game. I watched it and thought of you. You can soar with real eagles now.

Zuton Lucero-Mills

Zumante liked a lot of different things. When he was very small, he would watch football. He even seemed to understand it. He really liked the Denver Broncos. One day he decided that he also liked the Philadelphia Eagles. I was impressed by his individuality. I continue to be impressed.

December 1, 2009

This whole thing is so completely unbelievable. The images replay like a poorly written screenplay. I think that this is the type of story that I wouldn't finish. I would be disgusted by the apathy of the world, and absolutely unable to believe that such a thing could happen. I would throw the book away, not willing to think that a beautiful, spirited nine year old could be at the center of a cruel, heartrending tragedy. As it is, I am disgusted by the apathy of the world, unable to believe that such a thing has happened. I want to throw the book away. I am unwilling to believe that my beautiful, spirited nine-year-old son is at the center of this cruel, heartrending tragedy. I miss you so much. I pray each minute for peace, for strength, for courage, for understanding, for solace, for justice. I pray each minute for hope, for clarity, for guidance. I pray for the clock to rewind. I pray for history to be rewritten. I pray. And as I do, I mourn. I weep. I remember. I know that nothing is changing.

A great many things occurred as a result of Zumante's death. One is that I pray more—and harder, and longer, and more fervently. There has become so much to pray for, and about. In a world where I feel that an immeasurable injustice has been perpetrated, I must pray. It is one of the few things I have.

December 1, 2009

Four months ago you were buried. I think of that last day and I feel as though my chest is caving in. I think of your very last moment, when I laid my head on your chest and felt your last heartbeat, and I am crushed. I didn't think you would do it. I didn't think that you could leave me behind. I didn't think that God would allow it. But you did it. You left me. God allowed it. I think that if he had known what it would do to me, he would have made a different choice. He is supposed to be all knowing, but maybe he didn't know this time. I am destroyed. I have dissolved. Each day is a bigger challenge than the last. The future stretches before me and holds no promise that I find appealing. How will I ever make it?

The harsh, painful reality of losing a child is that you feel as though you can't possibly make it. But the harsh, painful reality of losing a child is that is that you DO make it. Perhaps thankfully—perhaps not. But you make it. Inch by inch. Moment by moment. Step by step. Day by day. You make it.

December 2, 2009

I am continually doing things that I can't do. I keep getting up, and going to work, and taking care of things and people, and I can't do it. I feel so shut down. It is as if I have been powered down, with no potential for reboot. Each second is harder than the last. With each step my feet feel heavier. I don't want to do anything. I make a huge effort to feel about things as I once felt about them, but it doesn't work. My soul has been ripped to shreds. My heart has been shattered. I hurt to a depth that I never knew existed. Each moment, my capacity for pain grows. I miss you.

In the time since my son died, I have done a lot. I have somehow gone about the usual business of living in this unusual time. I have felt as though I died with Zumante. But the evidence suggests that I didn't.

December 2, 2009

A little while ago, your siblings were playing and fighting and they were so loud. The louder they became, the louder the screams in my head got. I stood there, frozen, unable to say or do anything. All I heard was the absence of your voice.

Becoming a parent alters your life to an astounding degree. I became accustomed to a life with lots of activity and the din of voices was forever present. This has not changed. My household is still active and there are a great many voices to be heard. Still, there is a difference. I feel no shame in noticing it.

December 2, 2009

I think being burned alive would be more bearable than this. NOTHING can possibly compare with the pain of having your child die.

There are many types of pain. In the course of a lifetime, we all experience some. I can make no claims about the pain that others have experienced. I can only speak of my own. My pain is the worst pain imaginable. Everyone's is.

December 2, 2009

I try really hard to be an easy person to be around. But every second of every minute of every hour of every day, I am suffering. And sometimes it shows.

When your child dies, people ask how you're doing. Often, they don't really want to know. The truth is too intense. However, there appears to be some sort of obligation to make inquiries of a grieving person. It is not my intention to make life difficult or uncomfortable for anyone else. I can't change the fact that it is for me.

December 2, 2009

All I want for Christmas is for my son to not be dead.

Like any mother whose child has died, I have wanted for it to not be so. I have expended a great deal of time and energy wanting it to not be so. It is so. I know it. But we all have things we want.

December 3, 2009

I can't even begin to put it into words today.

There are always a million thoughts in my head and a million emotions in my heart. I cannot always articulate them. The language I know is not always sufficient.

December 5, 2009

There is nothing that I do that does not include missing you. It takes my breath away. Yesterday, I found myself wondering why I was having chest pains. And as my heart pounded, and the walls closed in around me, I knew. My chest hurts because my life hurts.

Grief is not simply emotional. It is a tangible, physical thing. Grief can cause the body to have ailments previously unencountered. This is in no way unusual. There is nothing abnormal about it. It is part of the process.

December 6, 2009

I am still waiting for the moment when this makes sense.

It is only natural to look for the logic in life. Especially when the senses have been shocked and traumatized, the brain gropes in search of reason. There are times when reason is elusive. The death of your child is such a time. There is nothing about it that makes sense.

December 9, 2009

I am drowning.

Each day is a process. It can feel like drowning. Or treading water. An outsider may not notice. To them, you are still swimming. It's possible that you are—but the stroke is definitely different.

December 14, 2009

There have been other tragedies in my life. I have been blindsided. I have cried. I have questioned. I have been in pain. And then you died. And I would not hesitate for a moment to relive every single one of those past experiences a million times over if it would restore you to me. And I would smile. I would face it bravely, knowing what my reward would be. Please, God. Can't we make a deal?

I have put many deals on the table for God's consideration. He has not taken me up on any of them. I know that he won't. That knowledge won't keep me from trying. I feel like if I did, I would be giving up on my son. What kind of mother just gives up on their child?

December 17, 2009

I find all of this simply infuriating. You didn't have to die. I wish desperately that I could sustain this anger, but I can't because the grief keeps overcoming me with the force of a tidal wave. I just feel so confused and so lost. I can't do this anymore. But I'm trying.

Sometimes, dealing with death makes you angry. The anger can be welcome, because of all the emotions possible, it feels a bit more manageable. Anger allows one to rant and rage, to curse and howl and bellow. When it abates, the sadness does not feel useful or manageable. It can make you feel incapable of going on. Then another day begins.

December 20, 2009

It hurts my feelings to be planning Christmas. I didn't know that last year would be my last Christmas with you…I'm sorry son.

The anticipation of the first Christmas without Zumante absolutely killed me. I kept thinking about the last Christmas we had with him. Should I have done more? Could I have made it more special? I wanted to apologize for not knowing—for it just being a "regular" holiday affair. Now I feel like "regular" was pretty good.

December 21, 2009

It has been five months since you died. Every day I come to this website and stare at it. I am often immobilized. I try to put into words what I am feeling, and I can't. It seems unthinkable that time is passing. Yesterday it was summer and you were doing the Jerk. We were talking and laughing. Everyone was having so much fun. And it is winter now. Earlier we decorated the Christmas tree without you. It was beautiful and I cried because you didn't help. Since 1999, I have shared Christmas with you. And I can't stop.

When someone you love dies, it seems odd to think of the passage of time. You can feel so stuck that you anticipate the entire world pausing in sympathy. It doesn't. The seasons continue to change. Life doesn't stop. Neither does remembrance. However it happens, we continue to involve our loved ones in our experiences. That's how it should be.

December 22, 2009

Another day. How I miss you.

Throughout everything, missing Zumante has been a constant. It has not ebbed or abated. It is one thing I can count on. There is no need to question it. As long as I have breath, I will miss my son.

December 24, 2009

These days are so very hard. I thought that you dying was the worst that could happen, but living without you is torture. The other day, I caught myself wishing that the end of the world would just hurry up and come, because then I wouldn't have to worry about the rest of my life, and everyone I love would be together again. It is the only resolution that I can think of. And I'm pretty sure that it isn't going to work out that way.

It bothers me that I can't figure out a way to reconcile this situation. It's only human to want to solve a problem. Death, however, is a problem that has no solution. And so, until the end of the world actually comes, I will continue to make my way through difficult days and try to find meaning in it all.

December 24, 2009

Christmas is fast approaching and I am a mess. It bothers me that I will never know what would have been on your list this year. I don't know how I will make it through the day.

When Zumante died, I resolved that I would still keep pace with him. I think about how tall he would be today, and how his interests might have changed. I observe the way his peers communicate. I ponder what his dreams might be. I will never know—but I'll always consider the possibilities.

December 24, 2009

When I was little, and I cried over something unnecessary, my grandma would tell me that I should save my tears for something important. Otherwise, there would come a time in my life when I needed tears and I wouldn't have any. Well, I heeded her words, and I have plenty of tears for you.

Zuton Lucero-Mills

I have shed more tears than I ever imagined I could. It sometimes surprises me that I haven't become dehydrated due to the loss of fluids, or floated away in a sea of devastation. It doesn't feel like it in the midst of despair, but tears have healing power. Through my tears, I anticipate some healing.

December 25, 2009

I have always loved Christmas. For as long as I can remember, giving has been something that has given me immense pleasure. Christmas has been special to me not just because of the sights, and sounds, and smells, and tastes, but because it is an occasion when I can give to my heart's content. Having that first child to give to took me to a whole new level of joy. And now, that first child has been taken, and I am baffled. I am still giving, but I am not content. I want someone to give me my son back.

It is a fact that no matter how badly I want it, Zumante will not be returned to me. In life, he gave me so much. Joy. Laughter. And memories. His death gave to me also. It gave me a mission. As a result, my giving has been altered. I will still give myself to Zumante. Somehow, he still gives to me.

December 29, 2009

I don't think I will ever understand any of this. Just moments ago, your brother was remembering the "Mante" doll that they were given in the hospital. They bandaged the doll and did their best to make it better. And still—with all of their hopes—you died. And I packed up your ICU room, taking the pictures and drawings from the walls, the stuffed animals from your bed, the cards from the table. I gathered the balloons. I went home and went to bed and early in the morning I went to your room and fell to my knees and cried. And I kept saying your name, and it didn't help. And I went to the hospital and your room was empty. And none of this makes any sense. This has got to be a mistake. This cannot be how this was supposed to happen.

Having my son die made me closely reexamine my beliefs. I have always believed that things generally happen the way that they're supposed to. I have believed it firmly and deeply. Now, though, it is sometimes a struggle to believe that. But I do. I keep telling myself that I haven't been wrong my entire life. I just have to figure out what's supposed to happen now.

December 31, 2009

I cannot wait for this year to be over. It has not been kind to me.

I was not sad to see 2009 end. Too much pain had been felt, too many trials experienced. I wanted the year to be over. I thought surely a new year would be less cruel. We're always hoping for something better.

December 31, 2009

It is twenty minutes until the New Year. We are having a party over here. Everyone dressed up and we have trays of hor' dourves, and a general merriment is in the air. I am pleased with the atmosphere I have created. I need to celebrate on this night. Thank goodness this year is ending. I can say goodbye to the year that has stolen my son from me. Good riddance. Hurry up 2010. You have to be better than what has already been.

At our New Year's Eve party that year, it was all about the fun. I slipped away a couple of times to reflect. For the rest of my life, when I think of 2009, I will recall it as the year my son died. He couldn't die again in 2010. That automatically made it better.

December 31, 2009

I wish for justice in the New Year. I wish for peace. I wish for strength. I wish for courage. Countdown. Let the ball drop already.

In the last moments of 2009, there was so much that I thought of and hoped for. I'm still waiting for my hopes to be fulfilled. It is about more than wishing. Wishes don't just come true. You usually have to work for it.

Through the storm...

My family has always been close. When I was growing up, it was common to eat dinner together. We went on family outings, and played games together. We talked to each other.

This did not change when I reached adulthood. We still had time for each other. We still managed to have some meals together, and we still scheduled outings for the entire group. We still enjoyed friendly competition.

I have never had to go looking for my family. I've not had the experience of wishing we were closer, nor have I gone weeks, or even days, without being in contact with someone. My family is my safe haven.

On July 15, 2009, the day before Zumante's final asthma attack, my family and I were together. It was a birthday celebration, and we had a grand time. The kids played games in the backyard, and we ate. There was a lot of laughter.

There was conversation about everything and nothing. The weather was nice. My dad took pictures.

Such is my family portrait. The next day, when my life changed forever, I called on my family. I didn't need to unearth their phone numbers from long forgotten address books, or wonder if they would come when I called. We didn't come together grudgingly because there had been a tragedy and, therefore, there was no other choice. In fact, it was quite the opposite.

My mother, whose number I had on speed dial, was the first one I called. The first thing I said to her was "Mom, I need you." She didn't hesitate, and I knew she wouldn't. The family came together without incident. It's no wonder. After all, we were never apart.

I know how fortunate I am, and I have thanked God repeatedly for my family. There is no question that grief is a horrendous process regardless of the circumstances, yet I am positive that, for me, the process has been less horrific because of my support system. I cannot fathom how people navigate grief without one.

January 1, 2010

I think of you dying and I just ache. My stomach twists itself in knots and I try to take deep breaths, and nothing helps. I don't get it. How could the world lose such a beautiful spirit and keep turning? I want to scream. I don't know how I am supposed to keep living. It doesn't feel like I really am. Somehow, I am existing. My system refuses to shut down and I am forced to endure the cruelty of my being alive and your being dead. What a way to live.

Life after the death of your child is hard. There is no getting over it, no getting around it. You can only go through it. It's no way to live. But there are no other options.

January 1, 2010

Today I bought a battery operated pencil sharpener. I know that this does not seem like a big deal, but it feels like one. As I was driving home, I thought of how you loved to draw. You would have been excited to be able to keep your pencils sharp. I wonder if "little" things like this will always hurt so much. Right now, it cuts like a machete. I am just bleeding and bleeding and there are no band-aids or stitches or sutures that will repair this wound. It is all so unbearable, and bearing it is exhausting. It never occurred to me that one day, you would be free, and I would be a captive. Yet, that is fairly accurate. I am a captive to grief, to misery, to longing, to despair, to tears, to hurt, to anger, to frustration, to loneliness, to fear, to anxiety, to heartbreak. I don't know what my crime was. But I know that I have been sentenced to live the rest of my life without you. And it is so wrong and so unfair and I want to appeal and I have appealed and it seems that the decision stands. And I am falling, crumbling, crushed, beneath the weight of this burden. I keep saying that I miss you, and those words fall so short. I NEED you. Last night, I was so glad that the year was ending. Today, I am distressed. It is just the beginning of my first full year without you. What a mess.

Zuton Lucero-Mills

Emotions are ever shifting. On New Year's Eve, I felt relief. On New Year's Day, I felt despair. I don't know if it will always be this way. What I do know is that the emotions I felt right after Zumante's death I am feeling still. There's nothing wrong with it. It isn't abnormal. I accept it. I own it.

January 4, 2010

Nighttime is really aggravating. I hate going to sleep. I generally toss and turn, or else wake repeatedly. My dreams are strange. But it is the waking up that is the worst. As soon as I am conscious, my first thought is of you. And every awful detail rushes to the surface and I feel as though I have had the wind knocked out of me. And I have to begin the process of actually doing things. I hate that waking up moment. It's like every time I open my eyes, you die again right in front of them.

I am grateful when I have a night that's not awful. I used to talk about what a difficult time I was having at night, but the conversation was so redundant, I stopped mentioning it. This does not mean the issue has completely resolved. Zumante's death is not an issue that will resolve. But I believe he would want me to live. I'm doing my best.

January 6, 2010

I am tired. It takes so much effort for me to make it through a day. No matter what I do, it seems as though I am spinning my wheels. Nothing I do strikes me as very important unless it relates directly to you. I am utterly destroyed. When I think of you, I think of your life. And I think of your death. And I hurt more than I could ever explain. No matter what, I know that I will NEVER, in this lifetime, hug you again. And I can get tokens, or commemorate what would have been, and ultimately, nothing changes. I got you a birthday present and balloons, but you will never get to be ten except in my heart. You have new shoes that you won't get to wear. Christmas presents that I didn't get to see you smile over. You will miss your elementary continuation. You won't go to middle school. You won't graduate from high school or go on to college. You won't know the joy of getting married and having children and thinking about it all has me completely undone. I try SO hard to frame everything in the positive, but I can't find it today. I know it is out of character—it just doesn't fit me. But nothing else makes any sense either.

Zuton Lucero-Mills

Grief is exhausting. It is impossible not to ponder what could have, or would have, been. It's absolutely maddening. You turn things over and over in your mind and things just don't add up. I am trying to teach myself, without much success, to stop questioning. Sometimes the questions don't really matter—it's the answer that does.

January 12, 2010

It is hard to write. A little while ago I went looking for a book to read so that I could try to escape. The one that caught my eye was The Interruption of Everything. I thought that was fitting.

As far back as I can remember, writing has felt like my salvation. It's odd that now it can require such effort. Life has shifted quite dramatically. I recall vividly the day that I came across that book. I began to read, but soon put it down. When your child dies, it really does interrupt everything. I'm still waiting for the part where it picks back up.

January 12, 2010

Every second, I hurt more than I did the last. And sometimes I get so frustrated and mad. I wish God had the guts to stand in front of me and try to explain himself.

There are those that are appalled that anyone would dare be mad at God. But I am livid. I won't deny it. And I don't believe that God begrudges me my feelings. I think he gets it. I wouldn't write off one of my children for being angry with me. I'm confident that God won't either.

January 12, 2010

I have written and erased three times in the last five minutes. I give up.

Mommy's Reflections has been an outlet for me. I have needed a safe place to do whatever I felt like doing. It's important to create those corners in your life. There are times, though, when even the safe places lend no comfort. In those times, it's even more important to try to center yourself. And know that even as you are throwing up your hands in a show of surrender, the universe is shifting. It's aligning itself for the better times ahead.

January 15, 2010

I have discovered that a huge part of being a mom is that whatever your child feels, you feel magnified. I laughed when you laughed and cried when you cried. When you were hungry, my stomach grumbled. When you were sick, I needed medicine. When you hurt, I hurt worse. When you cut yourself, I bled. I am truly mystified now though. You are free, and I have never felt so captive.

There are points during the parent-child relationship when it is quite obvious that parent and child are separate people. When baby takes its first steps, autonomy is asserted. Clearly, this is a person with their own thoughts, abilities, and direction. This can be a bit of a difficult thing for a parent to accept. It can also be a source of great pride. When Zumante freed himself from my embrace to travel, unassisted, on shaky legs, I was proud. When he freed himself from my embrace to travel, unassisted, into death, I was destroyed.

January 16, 2010

We used to read all of the books that talked about how much people loved each other. And one would say "I love you up to the ceiling!" and another "I love you up to the moon!" We would come up with our own and try to outdo each other. Now, I play a solitary game of "Guess how much I miss you?" I can never find anything that goes far enough.

Zuton Lucero-Mills

There is no adequate means of describing how much I miss Zumante. In fact, even the word "miss" is insufficient. I use it because I have nothing else at my disposal. I am aggravated by this lack of sufficient vocabulary. Until I discover something else to say, I am left with the word "miss". I don't want to find a better way to express it; I just want the need to express it to disappear. It won't happen.

January 16, 2010

howthishurts

I have never broken a limb. I have not been burned beyond recognition or beaten to near death. I haven't been shot, or stabbed, or strangled. I don't know the pain of any of these things. Yet I feel confident in saying that my hurt surpasses all of them.

January 19, 2010

It is Martin Luther King Jr. Day. Last year, we went to the Marade and talked a lot about MLK and his famous dreams. This year, I am living in a nightmare and struggling with my own dreams.

I am a mother that talks to her children. As a result, I have had the privilege of really getting to know them and their hopes and dreams. I was excited about attending the Marade with my kids because I had the opportunity to talk to them about history, and what part they want to play in it. All children should have dreams. They should all have the chance to transform dreams into reality. Zumante didn't get a chance, and that hurts me to my core. When you are grieving the death of a child, you don't only grieve for what was. You grieve for what could have and should have been.

January 19, 2010

I have a dream. I have a dream that one day this will be a country whose citizens will all have healthcare. I have a dream that healthcare will not be awarded by virtue of race, class, or socioeconomic standing, but that this country will give it freely to all in the great name of humanity. I have a dream today. I have a dream that, one day, no more mothers will mourn the loss of their children who died prematurely, and unnecessarily. No more children will shed tears for missed siblings who would be present but for a lack of grace on the part of a flawed system. I have a dream that one day this nation will rise up and proclaim that no more citizens shall go without in the richest nation in the world. I have a dream today. I dream that my remaining children will hold their heads high with the knowledge that there will never again be a case like yours and I will cry "Justice at last—Justice at last. We fought the battles and won the war and we got justice for Zumante at last."

When I was very small, I had dreams. As I grew, my dreams did also. I have had the good fortune of realizing a great many of my dreams. But, out of the death of my child, some other dreams emerged. I don't just WANT for them to be realized. I NEED it.

January 22, 2010

Sometimes when I think of you being dead, all I can do is sigh. I try to process my thoughts, and I am simply exhausted. I feel so heavy, like a million pound weight has been attached to my feet, and I am dragging it around. I have two lives: one where you are alive and I don't hurt without ceasing and one where you are dead and I hurt even when I am happy. I am trying to carry on, because I know that I have things that must be done. You died. It makes me mad and breaks my heart that I have to live. I miss you.

Death is unwavering. When you are living with grief, you can expend so much time and energy trying to convince death to waver. It won't. It's a terribly harsh reality. What else is there to do but sigh? So that is what you do. You sigh, and keep moving.

January 22, 2010

I am sick and tired of all of this reflecting. I wish I didn't have so much to reflect about.

Before Zumante died, life was very full. There were many things to do, and always plenty to think about. That has not changed. Life is still full, and I am still doing. Yet, in the midst of it all, I am thinking of Zumante. I analyze his life and his death. I reflect on how his life and death have affected my life. There is no end to these thoughts. I don't expect that there ever will be.

February 1, 2010

It is getting harder for me to write. I am so consumed with thoughts of you that it is hard for me to form a coherent sentence. I hope you understand. I miss you.

I became a writer at a young age. Writing has been my joy. Sometimes it has been my salvation. I appreciate the power of writing. It has kept me sane. The power to write is not always with me though. In my darkest hours, I am sometimes stripped of my ability to write. Unfortunately, when your child dies, you lose more than just your child. Parts of your being can crumble. I don't want to lose myself too. I'm going to keep struggling so that doesn't happen.

February 6, 2010

"Promise me you'll always remember: You're braver than you believe, and stronger than you seem, and smarter than you think."
Christopher Robin (Winnie-the-Pooh)

I am trying so hard…

At a moment when my need was most desperate, my sister presented this quote to me. I often repeat it to myself. I'm not always convinced, but it is true. I am brave, and strong, and smart. I just get sick of it sometimes. How brave, how strong, how smart, must I be?

February 6, 2010

The grass is green,
The sky is blue.
The birds still sing,
Yet I'm without you.
Life goes on,
I didn't think it would.
The world still turns,
And you're gone for good.
This poem hurts,
Just because…
Everything is the same,
Yet not as it was.

Zuton Lucero-Mills

I am shocked and amazed at the world around me. I wonder at the grass for growing, and at the sky for maintaining its hue. I ponder deeply the song of the birds, and the rotation of the earth itself. There are moments when I take it all very personally. I observe without enjoying. Death is a deep wound. I don't know how long it bleeds.

February 7, 2010

This is so hard.

Lots of things are hard. Sometimes things in school were hard. I have had hard conversations. There have been hard decisions. But this—this is more than hard. This is shattering, and debilitating, and mind-boggling. Hard. I much prefer the hard I had before.

February 16, 2010

Yesterday, one of the kids hugged me and I felt the absence of you. Life feels surreal. I have heard many times, that time eases the pain, that it has healing power. I don't believe it. Each grain of time is only another space to ache in. Time does not heal. Time hurts.

At the time of this writing, I have not grown any fonder of time. I generally consider it to be an enemy. I find the passage of time to be frustrating. I was absolutely assured that it has healing properties. Yet, no one can tell me when this change will occur. What I do know is this: eventually the time will come that I get to reunite with my son. I'm waiting.

February 25, 2010

I dreamed of you. Even in the space of my dream, I knew that you were dead, and I was pained. I was so grateful to see you alive, running, but I also felt like I was being teased without mercy. My son. I am hoping you visit me in my dreams again.

I never before had dreams that were so vivid. The colors are vibrant, and everything is sharply in focus. It's remarkable. At times, my dreams are more lifelike than my reality. When Zumante visits me in my dreams, I am ambivalent. I need to see him so badly, but it pains me so deeply. Still, every time I close my eyes, I pray to see my son. I wish my prayers were answered more often.

Through the storm...

I adore children. As a young child, my first aspiration was to be a mother. Eventually my dream expanded to include working with children in a formal setting. I've had very few dreams that didn't somehow involve kids.

I began working in an elementary school while still in high school. Over the years, I've worked with newborns through middle schoolers. I love my work. I think I was meant to do it.

The school year before Mante died, I was working mostly with kindergarteners in an elementary school. I found that I liked the adults in the building as much as the children. I rose in the morning excited about the prospect of work, and departed at the end of my workdays still feeling good.

Work was more than work. I was invested in the children, I cared about my coworkers, and felt that they also cared for me. They became my school family.

Even though Zumante died during the summer, and school was not in session, I immediately thought to contact my coworkers.

Less than a month after Mante died, and within days of the 10th birthday he didn't live to see, school started. I was questioned by many about whether I intended to return to work. I honestly never even considered anything else.

I went back to work in a fragile state. There were days when I was in tears when I entered the building. There were times when I sat in the school psychologist's office trying to put my feelings into words. There are moments when I knew that my despair was clearly on display. My coworkers checked in with me often. They cried with me. They talked with me and listened to me. They held me up when I was falling down. They knew when to be hands on and when to give me space. They provided calm in the midst of my storm.

March 5, 2010

Life has changed so much. In an instant, the world shifted. Its turning is making me dizzy. I wish it would stop and let me off.

It is astounding that my entire life was altered in the space of a heartbeat. It is beyond comprehension and explanation. It's as though I exited a dizzying amusement park ride and found everything topsy-turvy. I am queasy. I want the ride to end. Could it be that it's only just begun?

March 7, 2010

I smiled as I thought of you,
But then I had to cry.
I'm so amazed by the life you had,
Yet, parts of it just make me sigh.
I smiled today as I thought of you,
The beauty that you brought to my life.
I'm angry at the chain of events,
The unnecessary agony and strife.
I smiled and smiled as I thought of you.
And I cried and I cried and I cried.
Much as I did bringing you to the world—
I smiled and cried when you died.

Zuton Lucero-Mills

Everything is a contrast—an exercise in joy and sorrow. I cry through my laughter, and laugh through my tears. There is so much that Zumante gave me to smile about. There is so much to cry about. I doubt I'll ever stop doing either.

March 10, 2010

We had spaghetti for dinner tonight. It was one of your favorite foods. You used to shovel it in so fast. I remember that I finally sat down with you and showed you how to twirl the noodles on your fork. You were proud of your new skill, and I was relieved that the new method slowed you down a little bit. I'm enjoying this memory. So far, I have smiled without crying.

I've always had a great memory. It's not unusual for me to be teased about the magnitude of things that I remember. In the wake of Zumante's death, my memory has been a blessing and a curse. I have cried rivers as a result of being overwhelmed by memories, and my heart has soared because of them. Memories are good. I hope they never leave me.

March 22, 2010

Bill for health care reform just passed. Too late for you…but others?

There is a tremendous amount of debate around health care reform. I watch and listen and think of Zumante. I hope that one day there isn't so much to debate. Perhaps society will choose to be humane.

March 24, 2010

I am never able to think of you without sighing. I hope, always, that from your death there will emerge a greater good. But even in the midst of this thought, another thought rises to the surface—screw the greater good, I just want my son.

I try to stay focused. When I think of Zumante's death, I am ever mindful that, perhaps, it will lead to change. Maybe another child's life will be saved. On the other hand, why couldn't his life be the one that was saved? Does the way really have to be paved by my child's passing?

March 24, 2010

There is supposed to be an answer tomorrow. What could they possibly say?

I am seeking answers. I have done so much questioning and the answers are few and far between. They are also insufficient. What I am slowly coming to realize is that I will have to get some of the answers from within. Asking of others isn't working.

April 14, 2010

I felt led to this place tonight. It has been a long time since I have been here. It is a hard place to be. It is not sufficient to say that I am hurting. It is a gross understatement to say that I miss you. The space that I live in is the agony of despair. Everything is so exciting right now, and there is so much to look forward to… but what is glaring to me is your absence—and when I look forward, it is with the heart-shattering knowledge of what I can't look forward to. It is cruel and inhumane to have to live once your child has died. God should be ashamed of himself. I don't know what the thought process could possibly be. No matter what supreme joy may be in store for me, it will never be enough to erase this. I am having a hard time talking myself through this tonight. I miss you son. Thanks for nudging me to come here.

On April 14, 2010, I was preparing for my wedding. There was a whirlwind of activity. I planned, and talked, and laughed. I agonized, and lamented, and cried. My joy will always be tempered by my grief.

April 14, 2010

I have a difficult time remembering life before death.

My life has been divided into two distinct segments. There is “Before Mante Died” and there is “After Mante Died”. Everything falls into one realm or the other. It is hard to remember before. It’s hard because I know that there can be no return to that time. “Before” was far too short. “After” seems infinite.

April 24, 2010

Good morning son. It is six-thirty am on wedding day. Before I even opened my eyes, you were on my mind. The weather today is supposed to be cloudy and raining until just before ceremony time. As I looked at the forecast, I pondered whether you and God are huddled together, lamenting the fact that you are not here. Perhaps that was you howling like the wind last night, having a tantrum to show your displeasure. Maybe the biting chill was you also, cold to match your mood. I wonder if you were each thunderclap and lightning bolt, as the angels tried in vain to calm your fury. Was each drop of rain a tear you shed because your grief was so immense? I understand. And I want you to have peace and joy on this day, knowing that you are not forgotten. Your part in this is of huge magnitude—thanks. I love you. So on this gray morning, I still have a song in my heart. It is this one:

You are my Mante, my only Mante
You make me happy when skies are gray
You'll never know son, how much I love you
Please don't take my Mante away

I will be watching for you.

I had a beautiful wedding. Everyone looked gorgeous. The children were all in the wedding party. All—except for Zumante. His best friend walked in his place and I am satisfied that he would have wanted it so. That morning, before I began my final preparations, I pondered and prayed. All day, I watched for Zumante, and all day he was evident. I won't forget him. I believe that he won't forget me either.

Through the storm...

At the time of Zumante's death, I was working at a daycare center. The evening of his last asthma attack, I called my supervisor and told her the circumstances. She told me to take whatever time I needed, and said to let her know what the daycare could do. It was a relief knowing that I wouldn't have to worry about one more thing. I made many calls during Mante's hospital stay, and each added a measure of support. I was so glad to have it.

I had been employed by the daycare for a while. That summer of 2009, I was working with school-aged children.

I was having so much fun with them. In particular, I was thrilled at spending so much time with my older children. I got to have quality time at home and at work. I smiled a lot.

While Zumante was in the hospital, there was no smiling. At the time, I didn't really reflect on what a joyous experience the summer had been. Eventually, though, I began to reflect a great deal.

The daycare director and manager came to the hospital. They assessed the situation and immediately began to brainstorm a way to make things easier. They coordinated

schedules and arranged for the other children to be accommodated at the center. The kids even spent the night with them immediately after Mante died so that I would have more time before facing them.

I knew that the situation was serious, but I never anticipated that Zumante would die.

When he did, I was astonished by what the daycare did next. They planned and executed an entire benefit. Between the three centers in the network, there were memorial t-shirts and a banner printed, and dinner organized. Countless people came together out of love for Zumante and support for us. It was a beautiful display.

It boggled my mind. I was floored. It was extremely touching that so many people went to such great lengths out of love. I won't ever forget it.

May 3, 2010

Went to the cemetery today and there was a burrow with three baby bunnies in it. Wow.

Each of the children in my house has a number given to them based on their birth order. Zumante is number three. In the three weeks before his death, we had to rescue three baby bunnies at our home. On Mante's headstone, there are three bunnies. The day that we discovered three baby bunnies in a burrow near his grave, my heart was full. When our loved ones leave us, they are never really gone. There are signs of them, like kisses from heaven. I hope Zumante never stops sending kisses.

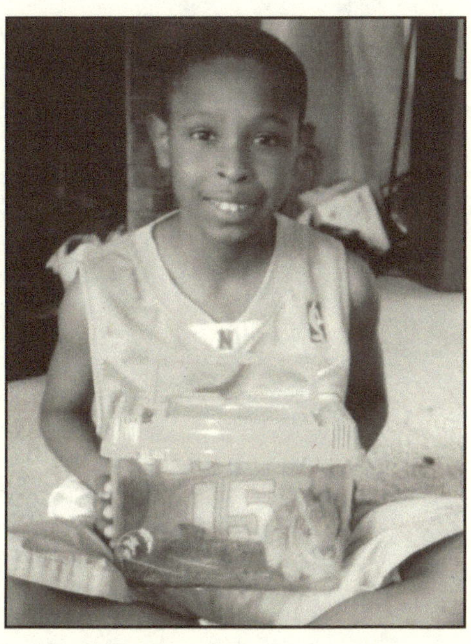

May 7, 2010

My first Mother's Day without my son is rapidly approaching and my heart hurts so badly. I didn't realize how hard this would be.

It is hard to face the "firsts" after the death of your child. Some are recognized by all as significant—first Christmas, first birthday. Only the grieving mother recognizes others. They all hurt terribly. There is no escaping the pain. You don't get over it. You get through it.

May 22, 2010

I want to be like you when I grow up.

Zuton Lucero-Mills

Most of us seem to recognize that our job as parents is to teach our children. I quickly learned that my children were also teaching me. I learned a lot from Zumante. I hope that one day he is as proud of me as I am of him.

May 22, 2010

What a difference a year makes.

Life has changed drastically. They have not been changes that I expected or welcomed. I deal with them. I don't feel like there's any other choice. The reality is that life is full of changes and challenges. I choose to focus on my response.

May 27, 2010

Yesterday was continuation,
And I awoke with dread.
I knew you couldn't cross the stage,
For you are lying dead.
Your friends arrived in Sunday best,
The air was alive with joy.
I felt like I would crumble,
Under the weight of missing my boy.
I sat and listened to fourth grade sing,
"If I Could Change the World".
It didn't change while I sat there,
I prayed but it still unfurled.
My heart was breaking more and more.
I couldn't stop the tears.
And when they called your name, and you didn't rise,
It was the sum of all my fears.

Zuton Lucero-Mills

Zumante's formal education began in preschool. When continuation day arrived, I fairly danced in my excitement. His hat was too big—or was it his head that was too small? No matter. I was proud. Kindergarten continuation came and we celebrated again. I was looking forward to fifth grade continuation. It would be the end of an era. Instead, he died after completing 4th grade and I accepted his 5th grade continuation certificate. Just because our children die, it doesn't mean that their accomplishments should. We still need to honor them.

May 27, 2010

Every day, in every way, I miss you more than words could say.

There is no adequate way to explain how deeply I miss my son. It is a yearning that surpasses definition. It is a hollowness that extends beyond the boundaries of time and space. It is an awful, debilitating, isolating feeling. How do you put it into words?

June 19, 2010

It has been 11 long months since you died... The other night, I sat in the basement alone and watched Dreamgirls. I was glad no one was there to see me cry. Every scene brought with it a memory, a thought. So I watched and cried, and cried and watched. I remembered. And even as the images played across the screen, a movie played in my head, and I wished with all of my heart that I could just turn it off. I heard you screaming and I wanted to scream too. I thought about how all of you kids used to pretend to be the characters and act out the entire movie—and how we would listen to the CD in the car and it was all so much fun and it is not fun now and I never thought I could be so miserable.

I have some fantastic memories. I'm glad I have them. I enjoy my memories. I think often of the fun I had with Zumante, and the fun we had as a family. Sometimes the fun and happy memories hurt my feelings. I wish Zumante were here so we could create more.

June 23, 2010

I have been straining so hard to hear your voice that it feels like my ears are bleeding. My arms are sore from all the hugs I haven't been able to give you. My soul is shattered from all the time I've spent without you. I miss you so. My life hurts.

Grief work is excruciating and tiresome. The pain is mental, physical, and emotional. The entire process is an aggravation. And yet… I know that I am grieving because I love Zumante. His life was a beautiful gift. It hurts now. But I would prefer to have the pain. Otherwise, I wouldn't have had the gift.

Through the storm...

Near the end of my pregnancy with Zumante, I had an appointment to interview a "prospective" pediatrician. By the time he had introduced himself and told me about the office, we had formed a firm friendship.

Over the years, we laughed together. We traded stories about our children. He saw me through all of my kids and all of their milestones. And, in the end, he helped see me through a death.

I called Zumante's pediatrician from the emergency department. He was hours away. He still came. He conversed with the other doctors, and sat with the family. He honestly answered my questions, and raged right along with me. He was there as he had always been. A relationship that had always been strong grew even stronger.

He hugged me. He held my hand. He kept watch with me. He cried. He, and his entire staff, attended Mante's funeral. He even spoke at the service.

I want to be clear that he was, and is, more than "just a pediatrician." I consider him a friend—family even. Zumante was so fortunate. I believe his doctor feels fortunate too.

Zuton Lucero-Mills

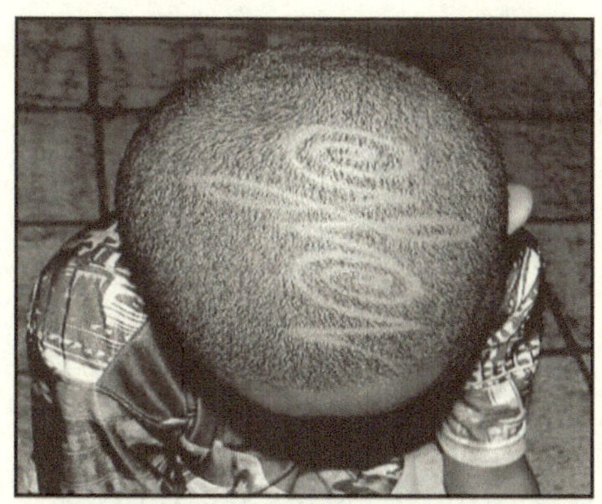

July 1, 2010

I thought of you so much today,
This was nothing new.
And as I thought of you, I wondered…
"Is he thinking of me too?"

I think of Zumante a great deal. I think not only of the time he spent living, but also of the time since. I wonder what he's been doing. I ponder whether he journeys with us during car trips, or checks on his siblings at school. Is he thinking of me? I believe he is.

July 10, 2010

If I hear one more time that God is good, I'm afraid I will scream.

It's not that I don't know that God is good. I know that. I get up every morning, I have food to eat, and clothes to wear, and a home to live in. I have friends and family. I have so much. But when your child has died and you are left behind, it is a challenge. When your 13 year old keeps drawing pictures in memory, and your 9 year old is angry all the time, and your 7 year old forever needs a hug (and he used to abhor them), when your 5 year old is too sad to eat dinner, and your 2 year old regularly asks to go to the cemetery... when you cry because you are always hurting, and eat because you are always empty... when you can't think of anything, but can't help thinking of one thing... when your soul and spirit are so battered and raw that sometimes you can't even move... well, it can be hard to think of God as being good. Seems pretty heartless to me.

Zuton Lucero-Mills

God and I have become closer. We have built an open and honest relationship. I count my blessings and thank him, and I also examine my trials and question him. It does not make me less of a believer. I go to God with my praise. I go to God with my fears. I go to God with my anger. I go to God with my questions. Even in my grief, I go to God. I have faith that he understands and accepts all of it.

July 16, 2010

One year ago today you had your very last asthma attack. Somehow, the thought does not make me breathe freely.

Asthma is an enemy of mine. I spent many years battling against it, determined that it would not claim my child. In the end, though, asthma was the victor. Zumante's last attack was terrifying. When it ended, Zumante lay limp in my arms, with his lips turning blue. The moment brought no relief. Just because something is over, does not necessarily mean that it is finished. When it comes to the matter of death, the moment of dying is most certainly not when it is finished. If you are the one left behind, that is when it begins.

July 28, 2010

I spend a great deal of time and energy trying to make sense of all of this. And no matter how I turn it over in my head, there is no sense in any of this. I feel so defeated. It is as though I have fought a million battles and lost them all and I am still forced to continue the war as though it may change something. Every moment this gets harder. Sometimes I have to remind myself to breathe. I concentrate really hard to do things that should require no thought at all. A lot of the time, there is very little that matters to me. I am sick of this. I don't want to play anymore.

Death is many things. Sensible it is not. My crusade for the sense in Zumante's death has yielded nothing. It won't. Knowing this, accepting this, is a trial. But I do know and accept it. I can't declare a game over simply because I would prefer it to be so. I will keep on struggling, keep on fighting, even through my apparent defeat. My reward won't come to me here. But it will come.

July 28, 2010

I pray a lot. I haven't gotten any answers that I can use.

It is not true that my prayer has yielded no useful answers. I sometimes feel that way. Feeling is not necessarily reality. In this case, the reality is that I have gotten answers to prayers. The answers have deviated from my wants and expectations. Still, they are useful. I'm trying to train myself to remember that.

July 28, 2010

It never made sense to me before how people could think that life was so awful that they just wanted to die. It makes perfect sense now.

Suicide has never held any appeal for me. I've neither tried it nor considered it. I think it's safe to say that I have also not really understood it. Bad things happen. People fail. Circumstances are less than ideal. It is truly awful when your child dies. I don't wish for death—but now I understand the sentiment.

July 28, 2010

I'm tired of lighting candles. I wish I could light the world on fire instead.

Having a website for Zumante is therapeutic. Helpful. Healing. Important. I have gone to the site and felt comforted. Soothed. Peaceful. I have made entries and felt useful. Productive. I have noted the love in the pages and felt inspired. Even powerful. However… There is a time when I feel none of this. Nothing feels good, or right. Part of grief is acceptance. It is the acceptance that life won't be the same.

July 28, 2010

I am furious with God tonight. I can't wait for judgment day so we can trade places and he can stand before me.

I have made no secret of my anger. There have been occasions that I raged at God and became angrier because he didn't defend himself. I look to God in my anger and I want to punish him because I feel punished. When my anger quiets, I find some clarity. My son died. God's son died too. That puts him in a position to know what I'm feeling.

July 28, 2010

so I am having a really bad day and nothing is helping

There are some bad days. There are also some really bad days. When they happen, sometimes all you can do is wait it out. Take it step by step or inch by inch or moment by moment. Some days are worse than others. It's okay. Even bad days eventually come to an end.

July 28, 2010

In this moment, when my world is so dark, I am struggling desperately to have faith… I am gritting my teeth and trying to be a mustard seed…

The Bible says that "If ye have faith as a grain of mustard seed, nothing shall be impossible unto you." I am a believer. I am a mother too. When Zumante died, my faith was shaken and tested. It continues to be. Somehow, though, I am still trying. I yell when need be, and cry when I have to. I crawl when I can't walk. I utilize my supports. And at the end of the day, no matter what, I remember the mustard seed.

Through the Storm...

The community at large has reached out to us. We received condolences from everyone from preschoolers to legislators. Complete strangers stopped us on the street to say that they had heard Zumante's story and were touched by it. My journey has not been solitary. No journey should be.

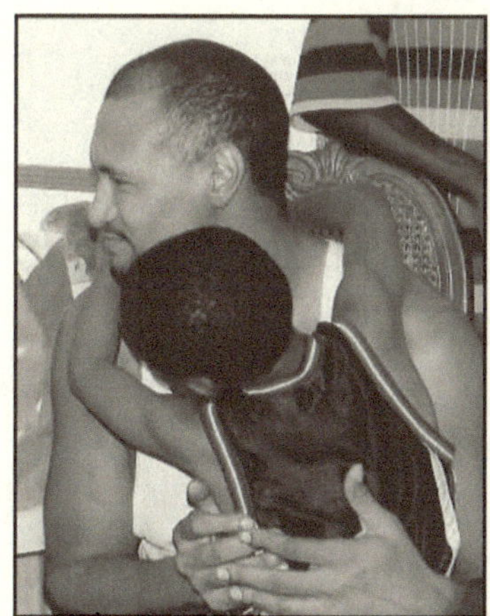

CHEER

August 1, 2010

Your body has been buried for a year now. My memories never will be.

Every day, I remember Zumante. This book is my attempt to honor that memory. I am his mommy, and these are my reflections. My wish is that others will also remember and reflect. Although we buried Mante's body, that is all that was buried. Everything else lives on.

Photo courtesy of the Denver Post.
Photographer Hyoung Chang.

www.ingramcontent.com/pod-product-compliance
Lightning Source LLC
LaVergne TN
LVHW050925080826
845145LV00001B/220

* 9 7 8 0 9 8 2 4 2 5 5 6 5 *